MW01173017

Understanding CHILDREN

A CONVERSATION

RABBI ABBA GOLDMAN, PH.D.

Organized by Rabbi Yehuda Zuckerman

First Printing March 2024

ISBN 979-8-8776-8189-7

Rabbi Goldman can be reached at:
(718) 887-6459

For book orders:
drgoldmanbook@gmail.com

Rabbinical Seminary of America

ישיבת רבנו ישראל מאיר הכהן זצוק״ל
בעל ה״חפץ חיים״
Dedicated by the Ginzberg Family

76-01 147th St., Flushing NY 11367
718.268.4700 / Fax: 718.268.4684
office@rabbinical.org

Rabbi Dovid Leibowitz זצוק״ל
Founding Rosh HaYeshiva 1933-1941

Rabbi A. Henach Leibowitz זצוק״ל
Rosh HaYeshiva 1941-2008

Rabbi Dovid Harris שליט״א
Rosh HaYeshiva

Rabbi Akiva Grunblatt שליט״א
Rosh HaYeshiva

Rabbi Shaul Opoczynski שליט״א
Rosh HaYeshiva

Dr. Ira Kukin ע״ה
Chairman Emeritus

Dr. Allan Jacob
Chairman of the Board

שבט תשפ״ד לפ״ק

שמחנו לקבל גליונות מתוך הספר "Understanding Children" , על ענייני
חינוך והדרכה להורים שנכתב על ידי הרב אבא גולדמן שליט״א, אחד מחשובי
תלמידי רבינו הראש הישיבה זצוק״ל. הרב הנ״ל למד הרבה שנים בישיבתנו
הק׳, ובמשך השנים, הדריך ועזר ונתן עצות למאות.

הספר מלא עצות והדרכות להורים ולמחנכים איך להצליח בחינוך הבנים
לחנכם ולהדריכם בדרך הטובה והישרה וללמד אותם מדות טובות ונאות,
ואיך להתנהג עם כל ילד וילד כפי מדתו הראויה לו. הרב הנ״ל ערך את
הדברים בטוב טעם ודעת לעשות נתיבות ללבם של ההורים ומחנכים כיצד
יוכלו להצליח במשימתם הגדולה לגדל ולחנך את אוצרם היקר מכל להיות
לעבד נאמן לד׳ ולתורתו.

הספר נכתב בשפה המדוברת במדינתנו ובעשייׂׂׂׂׂית תהי׳ לתועלת גדולה לכל
המעיינים בו, ולזה נחזיק טובא להרב המחבר שליט״א.

ולמרות שמחמת טרדות הישיבה לא הי׳ לנו פנאי לעיין בו כדבעי מ״מ אנו
מכירים היטב הרב המחבר שליט״א שהוא תלמיד חכם ובעל מוסר, ואינו
מוציא מתחת ידו דבר שאינו מתוקן. ואנו מברכים אותו מעומק לבבנו
שימשיך לזכות את הרבים, וימשיך עוד להפיץ מעיינותיו חוצה להגדיל תורה
ולהאדירה.

הכו״ח לכבוד התורה ולומדיי,

דוד הריס   עקיבא אליהו גרונבלאט   שאול חבל אופוצ׳ינסקי

Rabbi Goldman is available by phone
for clarifications and to discuss individual circumstances.
He can be reached at:
(718) 887-6459

Table of Contents

Foreword 1

The Essence of Chinuch The Nature of a Child 5

       Zeriah and Binyan 17

Chapter 1 Building Self Esteem in Young Children 24

Chapter 2 Holding Children 35

Chapter 3 Giving Attention 38

Chapter 4 Emotional Validation.. 45

Chapter 5 Routine and Structure 48

Chapter 6 Babysitters and Playgroups.. 51

Chapter 7 Preparing a Child for a New Baby............................. 59

Chapter 8 Caring for a Child with a Newborn Sibling................ 62

Chapter 9 Dealing with Multiple Children: Fighting, Sharing..... 66

Chapter 10 Children with Different Opportunities...................... 73

Chapter 11 Children Helping in the House 76

Chapter 12 Teaching a Child to Speak Nicely 81

Chapter 13 Temper Tantrums and Time-outs 83

Chapter 14 When to Hit a Child.. 88

Chapter 15 Physical Health of a Child 92

Chapter 16 Shabbos... 95

Chapter 17 Stories of Gedolim.. 97

Chapter 18 Sleep Training.. 99

Chapter 19 Sexuality in Young Children 107

Chapter 20 Pacifiers During the Day... 110

Foreword

With tremendous gratitude to Hashem, we present you with a book attempting to share Dr. Goldman's perspective and advice on the wonderful and challenging area of life which is parenting. For many years we had the privilege of having a weekly session with Dr. Goldman where we discussed many topics, which frequently included parenting. One member of the group had the idea that we should have a series dedicated to targeted areas, and that we should present the groups in written form so that others could benefit. This book is the product of that series of groups.

This book was not personally written by Dr. Goldman, nor is it a direct transcription. It is a compilation and organization of the thoughts he shared, which were put together into chapters. The chapters were given to and reviewed with him, to clarify aspects that were unclear to me when writing it. Dr. Goldman has looked over the entire manuscript, and has agreed that it be published under his name. That being said, the way that I wrote this book likely isn't exactly how Dr. Goldman would have written it himself, and the exact words I used may not be the ones Dr. Goldman would have picked. However, the basic ideas presented in this book accurately represent Dr. Goldman's perspective.

Some ideas are repeated multiple times in this book; frequently, they are core perspectives on parenting. Sometimes even important aspects of parenting are dealt with in just a couple of sentences. Thinking about each idea can help a person gain a healthy viewpoint. There are ideas which are dealt with over several discussions. In these cases, the reader is usually directed to the other pieces that deal with the related idea. Reading the book in its entirety will offer a more complete picture.

Many of the footnotes address questions that a serious reader may be troubled by. They are usually only written once, though the same question could be posed at a number of points. A reader who is troubled may find that a footnote many pages earlier dealt with their concern.

It is likely that the reader will find some ideas in the book to be novel and/or different from their current system of understanding. Though this may be a result of an implication that wasn't intended, or due to an error of mine in writing, it may be neither. The reader is encouraged to speak out the ideas with others; perhaps someone familiar with Dr. Goldman's perspective can explain the reasoning. Many ideas may be premised on ideas with which the reader may not be familiar. Readers can also reach out to Dr. Goldman directly to discuss. It is likely that with further thought one will come to understand the reasoning behind these ideas.

The format of this book includes questions that were posed to Dr. Goldman at the groups and the answers given by him. They were frequently left in a question-answer format to connect the reader to the learning experience more, particularly when the questions seemed to be about common ideas that many listeners and readers might wonder about. Despite the fact that not every question seems to have a logical premise, they were left in that format to aid in their presentation.

The focus of the groups and of this book is to help parents understand the basic principles for parenting children under two years of age. The original name for this book, 'Under Two Basics,' reflects that fact. In general, we tried to only include discussion that contributed to proper parenting of young children; however much of the content is also relevant to children above two years in age. In many areas, understanding how to parent older children is related to understanding how to parent younger children. Sometimes, we just couldn't hold ourselves back from putting it in.

Why was the book targeted to children under two years of age? One might think that there isn't much to say about parenting a child so young; wouldn't it make more sense to target children up to three years at least? I have asked this question myself. The answer is that this is *precisely* why it is targeted at that young demographic, to bring attention to, and focus on, the critical aspects of parenting very young children properly, so that they grow to become healthy children, teens, and adults.

There are many aspects to parenting, and they are interconnected. This book attempts to provide perspective on caring for children spiritually, as well as providing for their physical, emotional, and psychological needs. Parents must also be cautious not to neglect their own needs, or children will suffer along with them. Parents must have a way to care for their children while also caring for themselves.

Though this book was lightly edited with the helpful and kind assistance of Dr. Benjamin Miller, the complete contents of this book will be professionally edited in order to make it easier to read and process. We are publishing it first in a more natural form for the benefits which that form provides. While it may require more effort to understand the ideas presented, it is much closer to the way that

Dr. Goldman presents his perspective, and more fully preserves the words he chooses.

It is our hope that this book will help parents be more thoughtful in their parenting, so they can do their best to raise happy, healthy children. As the classic quote from our dear friend R' Ezzie (from the chapter on Giving Attention) says so nicely, "I may not be Dr. Goldman, but I'm trying to be." This is the proper perspective.

Yehuda Zuckerman
A Talmid

The Essence of Chinuch
The Nature of a Child

Parents play two basic roles in being *mechanech* growing children: they help children use their seichel, and they serve as role models of good middos and mitzvah adherence. Many people think that the way parents develop children is by causing a pattern of actions in their children by using reward and punishment. This is a mistake.

Why Children don't listen

R' Yaakov Kamenetsky would say that eighty percent of what is popularly considered chinuch is unnecessary. Children will do many proper things on their own, each thing when they reach a certain stage of development. Before children reach that stage, they either cannot understand specific ideas, or cannot follow through with them. After that stage is achieved, it no longer needs to be taught. Thus, most of what is done in the name of 'Chinuch' is actually not needed[1].

---

[1] R Yaakov's example for where parents have no role of chinuch is regarding children climbing on tables. When a child is young, they enjoy doing it, and cannot understand why they shouldn't climb on tables. When they get older, they understand, without

Children frequently disregard directives from their parents regarding the proper way to act. In a situation where children have a good relationship with their parents, this almost always happens due to either a lack of understanding about *why* they should act that way, a lack in their middos development, or a lack in their self-control.

Lack of Understanding

The Chovos Halevavos teaches us that there are two ways that a person inspires themselves to serve Hashem. There is the *heara* [inspiration/drive] of the *seichel* [the intellect] and the heara of the Torah. The heara of the seichel can be underestimated by parents. The seichel grows naturally, just as the body does, and there are certain things that the seichel understands simply due to its own growth, without requiring an explanation from the outside. (However, at each age, children can indeed be helped to understand certain more advanced concepts, even before they have reached the age at which these concepts would have come naturally, as discussed below).

Lack of Middos Development

Parents cannot directly help their children when the proper action involves the expression of a middah which a person must possess, as a part of their character, in order to demonstrate it. When a person has made mercy a part of his or her character, the person will express that middah of rachamim through acts of mercy. Middos are built into human beings. There is *no way* to explain *why* one should be a Baal Chesed, or *why* one should have mercy. Being forced to do acts of

---

any adult assistance, that a table is for eating, and understand as well that climbing on a table can ruin what is on it, as well as damage the table. There may not be any window of time in-between, where chinuch would have been helpful.

mercy when one does not yet have the middah[2] of rachamim as part of one's character, against one's will, will not help one grow in mercy. Parents cannot directly help children develop a middah through forcing its expression; what is required is for children to further grow, and the middah will naturally develop with time.

Lack of Self Control

When children *understand* the correct thing to do before they have the self-control needed to *act* on this understanding, parents cannot directly help[3] them to exhibit the necessary self-control.

Parents who attempt to instruct children on how to act properly, before they have the necessary self-control or middah development, or before they are able to grasp the understanding which is the basis of the action, will find their own middos tested, when the child repeatedly acts counter to the parent's teaching. [See footnote[4] as regards fulfilling one's obligation of chinuch]

---

[2] A middah is a motivation inside a person which is characterized by a feeling in a certain situation.

[3] Self-control is the seichel guiding the middos, which are emotions, showing the middos how to express themselves, and at times suppressing a middah and forcing it to not express itself. One grows in self-control as their seichel grows. One can also gain more self-control through learning Torah and recognizing our importance as a special people. When parents model self-control, children will want to be like them and also want to control themselves, as they do by middos. Another way to help a child grow in self-control is through making it fun or using the method under the heading 'Offering to help a child control themselves.'

[4] The mitzvah of chinuch in Orach Chaim Siman 343 is only applicable if the child has enough self-control that they are able to fulfill the mitzvah. It would be illogical for the Mishna Berura to say that parents should tell children about the obligation of a mitzvah before that point. Before children have achieved that developmental level, they will not only not do what they are told, but will feel guilty about it.

Helping a child use his seichel

Parents should help children in being able to use their already-developed seichel more effectively in order to serve Hashem.

Some ways parents can help children are:
1) Explaining to children certain ideas which they are capable of understanding, but are not yet aware of.
2) Helping children put logical pieces together and think through current situations.

Explaining ideas

Parents should teach children an explanation for each mitzvah (along with the idea that it is obligatory for adults) at an age where they can understand that mitzvah. Frequently, there is a window of time[5] during which children have the capacity to understand the correct thing to do with their own seichel, but cannot yet understand it without being helped by someone else. This is part of the first role of parents in being mechanech their children - helping them to understand.

Parents should explain the meaning of each mitzvah to children. Look up the Sefer HaChinuch so the mitzvah will have meaning and they will understand its significance[6]. Explain that adults *have* to do this

---

[5] The field of educational psychology also identifies this window, known as the Zone of Proximal Development (ZPD). First introduced by the psychologist Lev Vygotsky, the ZPD "represents the space between what a learner is capable of doing unsupported and what the learner cannot do even with support. It is the range where the learner is able to perform, but only with support from a teacher or a peer with more knowledge or expertise" (Penguin dictionary of psychology, Retrieved from Credo Reference database, 2009). -Dr. M

[6] Another drive for children to fulfill the mitzvos can be realizing that Hashem loves us and therefore we want to do what Hashem wants us to. A parent can help a child appreciate Hashem's love by pointing out the wonderful things Hashem does for us. In this way a child will come to love Hashem in return. A parent can point out that

mitzvah and that children should do it now, as practice, because when they grow up they will also have to do it very carefully.

For example, parents should explain to children that the reason why we only eat kosher food is because Hashem wants us to have special foods in order that we don't come to mix with the gentiles, as well as to realize that we are different. And on Shabbos we don't make changes to Hashem's world because Hashem made the world in six days and rested on Shabbos, so we celebrate the creation of the world by also resting on Shabbos.

Explaining an idea to overcome taavah's blockage to the seichel

Taavah [desire] develops prior to seichel, so children's taavah can block their seichel from understanding the correct thing to do in a given situation. Therefore, even though children will, on their own, have *some* understanding of how they should act, they may need outside help to understand the correct thing to do. Having parents explain the idea to them can help them gain more clarity, despite their taavah's efforts at blocking their understanding. (This assistance to the seichel may fall under the heara of the Torah.)

Putting logical pieces together

Parents should also help children work through situations, in order that the result will be them acting based on their own seichel. Social situations in particular are complicated. Many of those situations are discussed in **Multiple Children: Children Fighting**.

Sometimes children can understand an idea on their own, but require assistance in generalizing that knowledge to slightly different

---

Hashem made us a sun and a moon and put earth in the exact position for us to live. A parent can point out everything Hashem does for us each day.

situations. Parents can expand a child's understanding of stealing to include treating others' property with care and using them as intended.

Though at a certain age children can understand that speaking negatively about others can hurt those who are spoken about, they may not know *where* it applies. Children should be told the halachos of when lashon hara is assur and muttar when they have the necessary self-control and middos development (and ability to understand), that are the prerequisites for following those halachos.

Parents should explain to children how to act *in their own best interest*. At a certain age children can understand why eating too much of a certain food is not good for them, as it will make them sick to their stomach, and why one should wear a coat outside when it is cold, to avoid illness.

When parents explain to their children the *logic* behind how acting in a certain way is beneficial, they are doing something more for them than just helping them choose to make their life more pleasant. If parents were to *force* children to act in a certain way, even if the child's compliance would provide some immediate benefit to the child, they would feel invalidated, as if they are being treated like a servant, or a thing. Communicating with them by talking to their seichel is even more respectful to children than letting them do what they want (when it is against their own best interest). By explaining the logic to them, parents are treating children as human beings, with respect, and this is an important piece of building children's self-esteem.

Certain middah expressions have intellectual requirements

Often, we forget the heara of the seichel because we take it for granted. We forget the steps that are needed in order to do a mitzvah or exhibit a middah.

An example of this would be the drive to share one's possessions with others. There are multiple logical pieces to the urge of 'sharing'[7]:

1) To *understand* that other people have feelings. I experience my own feelings and I need to appreciate that other people also have feelings.

2) To know *what* those feelings are. A common way would be perspective taking; to put oneself into another's shoes; "How would *I* feel if *I* was in that position?" I wouldn't like to not have something and see another person with it.

Along with understanding those ideas, one must have developed the middah of chesed:

3) To think that If I don't like it, I want others to not have it either. The other person is my chaver. I like them. I do not want them to experience pain and suffering.

4) Therefore, I should take some of my own and give it to them so they don't feel bad.

These ideas are second nature to an adult, but beyond the grasp of a two- to three-year-old[8]. The instinct for expressing the middah of chesed may be there, but this expression has an intellectual component. The intellectual aspect will develop over time, and the middah will express itself unless resistance to the middah is cultivated.

---

[7] There is another logical reason to share, which parents more frequently give as the reason; because 'it is fair' to share. Fairness is the middah of emes, which develops in a child much later even than empathy and chesed, which comprise the reason given above.

[8] At that age, there is no chinuch to be done in this area. We are only trying to avoid the child harming others, while also trying to avoid harming the child. Some ways to do this are given in 'Multiple Children: Sharing.' At an older age, a parent may be able to assist a child in understanding the intellectual parts and in putting the pieces together. However, the middah of chesed, like all middos, cannot be explained.

Examples of helping children use their seichel

A good example of a parent's proper role is in the following story. A young boy didn't want to go to bed at bedtime. The father had many fun things planned for the next day, and explained to the child 'You will be very tired if you stay up, and won't be able to enjoy the fun things.' The father did not punish the child, instead he explained to the child a good reason to go to bed. The child cried and went to bed. The child understood that he has stayed up late before and has been tired. The child also understood that when he is tired, he has not enjoyed activities. The father reminded him[9] of these ideas, and connected the pieces for him. The child needs to both understand and have the self-control to be able to choose to go to bed.

Serving as a role model for children

For many years I had a question: "Why is there so little discussion in the Rishonim and Acharonim about chinuch?" This was until I saw an article written by Rabbi Keller. He wrote that the answer is that "Chinuch only involves two things: good middos and a bit of common sense." The parents having good middos is important, not just so that they don't get angry at children or deprive them of time and attention. Rather it is of utmost importance because children absorb middos from their parents. [One may notice a father walking with an unusual gait; all his children walk beside him, exhibiting the same gait. Children are naturally drawn to model their parents' behavior.]

All Jewish people are born with good middos which are undeveloped, but it takes some time for them to develop. Children are self-centered; becoming a baal chesed, being there for others and caring for them, takes time. Eventually it emerges. The only thing we can do in order

---

[9] Even adults forget with full clarity that staying up late will make them tired, and therefore have a tendency to stay up too late. They could use a reminder of this as well.

to develop children's good middos further is to manifest them ourselves.

The Rosh HaYeshiva zt"l's rebbetzin, Rebbetzin Pesha, was asked at what age parents should teach their children to say brachos. She responded that parents don't have to teach their children to make Brachos. 'Then how will they learn?' She said that if parents say brachos out loud, with kavannah, their children will naturally ask what they are doing. The children will then understand why brachos are meaningful, to be thankful to Hashem for all that he gives us, and the children will *want* to make brachos as well.

Children want to do what their admired parents do; they are anxiously eager to be like them. If their father is a fireman[10], they wish to be a fireman. If their father is a Ben Torah, they wish to be a Ben Torah.

Another aspect which parents can model for their children is an attitude about the importance of mitzvos and the seriousness of them. This will only be helpful for children after they understand a reason for the mitzvah, but after they understand one, it will heighten their appreciation for the mitzvah.

Offering to help a child control themselves

Parents should also offer to help children control themselves in certain situations. The first thing parents should try to figure out is *why* the child is not acting in the correct way to begin with. In many situations that is the route to addressing the incorrect behavior. If through discussion it comes out that the child wants to do the correct thing

---

[10] It is easier and more effective to inspire children to perform mitzvos by modeling them, in order to be like their parents, as they are specific actions, rather than middos which are personal characteristics. This is an additional reason why one should not force children to do mitzvos, since they will naturally do the mitzvos anyways in order to model their parents.

but finds him- or herself unable to control themselves, then parents could offer to reward the child for acting correctly. This is because it is cooperative, it is working together *with* the child. The child following through on this would be growth for the child because he or she is putting in their own effort. This child who wants to, can only be a child who has sufficient seichel to prompt them to want to (generally over six years of age at least). Rewards should not be used to motivate younger children unless there is no other way to accomplish something that is necessary for the child's own benefit[11] (rather parents should make the task fun so children will want to engage in it).

Rewards should be used to help children make up for the self-control that he or she is lacking, and therefore the reward should be proportionate only to make up for the missing self-control.

If a child just needs a little incentive, it can be done for young children[12] also, as long as there is not too much pressure being placed on them. One must be careful not to overload children. A frequent problem with star charts is that even if a child does want to do the actions (as before), the way they are typically designed and implemented involves asking the child to work on too many things at once.

Another caveat to parents using rewards to help a child control themselves is when the child is not yet interested in doing so. 'מכלל הן אתה שומע לאו,' [from the positive we see the negative]. If you offer a reward for an action, it must be because that action is good. The implication is that if they don't do it, then they are acting *bad*.

---

[11] Note for teachers: Sometimes rewards are a necessity for classroom management, which is necessary for the children and therefore proper. In addition, children frequently want to do the behavior which the teacher is offering to reward them for.

[12] One is unable to have the conversation previously presented with a younger child. When parents feel that their young child does want to perform something but doesn't have the self-control, they could offer a small incentive, for a shorter period of time. Keeping the incentive small will help ensure that the action is being done mostly out of the child's internal drive and not simply for the incentive.

Therefore, if a child ultimately chooses not to do the action, they will feel that the parent disapproves.

Providing opportunities where a child can choose to express a middah

All children are born with good middos, albeit undeveloped. Parents can help children choose to act in the same way as if the middah was being expressed, by making it fun, or by making the child feel grown up. The enjoyment is not a reward; rather it is a natural built-in benefit and therefore children will not feel forced in any way. They will be choosing to act just as the middah would be expressed, but with help. They will grow from the part of their intention to express the middah which has developed *to a degree*[13] within them. This is based on the principle of מתוך שלא לשמה בא לשמה [through acting driven by other intent, one comes to act for the proper intent] (See the footnote).

---

[13] The Rosh HaYeshiva zt"l explained that we only say מתוך שלא לשמה בא לשמה when one is intending to reach the level of לשמה [proper intent]. A person who is forced to act in a certain way only feels guilt, a fear of punishment, and the feeling that their צלם אלקים [free will] has been encroached upon, as they are being forced and cannot choose. They have no intention for this action to help them reach the level of לשמה. One who expresses a middah because it is fun, even a small child, has a low-level thought process that 'I want to help/be kind etc., and now I can in a fun way' and it is consistent with מתוך שלא לשמה בא לשמה.

By mitzvos, however, children who understand the meaning of a mitzvah will do it on their own. Doing a mitzvah without its understanding is not very meaningful and has a downside of מצות אנשים מלומדה as explained later. Therefore, in general, making the performance of a mitzvah fun, to encourage it before children understand the reason, is not a good idea. [See **Zeriah and Binyan** 'Binyan of a child by aveiros' for an exceptional situation.]

Forcing children to act beyond their understanding; Developing habits with reward and punishment

Forcing children to give up what they want, to act in a way that is beyond their understanding, will cause them to feel resentful and they may never perform the action with proper intentions. When children are forced to do anything, they feel invalidated as a human; that their *bechira* [free will] is being disrespected, and their resentment of that will prevent them from growing their middos through the experience. Parents can force behaviors and then lecture, but the result will be that children understand that their parents don't like what they are doing, without understanding the reason behind their parent's dislike of the action. Even if their parents do explain it to them, if they are forced to do the action, there can be a backlash. When middos or mitzvos are forced on children, they reject them.

Q: If children are forced to behave a certain way, will it be effective later in life?
Dr. G: It may be effective, but whether they act that way or they don't, there will be guilt and resentment.
For example, a woman can have great difficulty doing household chores, because she was forced to do them as a child. Even though she *understands* that the role of a wife is to make a home for her husband, she has an internal challenge to it. It can even prevent her from making important life decisions that she would want to choose, because they involve more housework than she feels able to do. Similarly, a boy who is forced to go to school and learn until late at night will resent that.

Even if one convinces a child by offering them a reward big enough that they feel forced to comply in order to receive the reward, if done for something that the child does not yet want to do, it is harmful to the child. The fact that the child ostensibly 'chose' the reward because of its benefit does not remove the feeling of having had their bechira encroached upon (they feel as if they had no real choice, given the size of the reward, and were therefore not truly able to choose). In addition, it is almost inevitable that parents will feel disapproval if children end up not acting how they want them to, and the children will perceive that disapproval.

We know from Chazal that there is an idea of being mechanech with a 'shevet [stick of] mussar.' Rabbeinu Bechaya in his *hakdama* [introduction] to Parshas Shemos explains that this refers to speaking gently and persistently. Parents should not give up if their attempts to address a child's issue have not resulted in change. Parents should instead discuss with the child ways for the child to control themselves, and try again to understand *why* the child is not acting correctly.

Zeriah and Binyan[14]

The idea of 'Binyan' by a person, building a person, is similar to how an assembly line in a factory functions. There is a plan as to where each piece goes; each piece is connected; all the products are the same; it follows the plan. Some people have a vision of educating children that way alone. They think that the way to 'Build a Torah personality' is by putting all the pieces together, in the same way for all children. "Everyone has to call Grandma each Erev Shabbos, or you are a bad boy;" "help Mommy set the table;" "no child insults Daddy." There are lists of Dos and Don'ts, shoulds and shouldn'ts. They believe that if children are put together according to the plan, using reward and punishment, then the result will be a Torah personality. That is how some envision Chinuch.

---

[14] These ideas are based on the sefer on chinuch by R' Shlomo Wolbe זריעה ובנין בחינוך, Planting and Building in Chinuch. What is presented is Dr. Goldman's understanding of them and how to apply them.

The idea of 'Zeriah,' growing a person, is similar to how a farmer nurtures a plant. The farmer prepares the soil by pulling the weeds, then he puts in the little seeds, and he hopes for sun and water. The seed isn't imposed upon, the way rewards and punishments do in children, coming from the outside. The seed grows from its inner nature, and the most the farmer can do is provide a good environment. The seed will become whatever it is destined to become.

Zeriah is the growing seichel; children are born with tendencies like an animal, lacking seichel. The seichel grows like a seed; just as the body grows, so does the seichel. Largely it grows from within.

Children still require instruction, as the seichel does not fully mature until adulthood. Productive use of Binyan is all the things parents can do to help children use their seichel more effectively. Principally, chinuch is comprised of explanations, which help children have more understanding for their seichel to act upon. It also includes the ideas of helping children put logical pieces together and work through situations, as well as provide certain opportunities for children to choose for themselves, by helping them control themselves when they want to do so, and by making expressing middos fun.

Binyan also includes practical routines to get things done that are in the children's best interest, but that they don't yet understand. Structure is an important facet that children require for healthy development, as it assists them in developing the middah of *seder* [orderliness][15]. It also helps make every part of the day fun and

---

[15] The middah of seder is unique. Because seder cannot be done as a thoughtful thing, one is unable to thoughtfully 'be neat' (it takes too much brain power to always act neatly). Therefore, one must make 'being neat' into a habit for oneself. This middah is one of creating the habit of orderliness. As an adult, one would do this by actively being neat at limited times, which will then generalize into a habit of neatness in both that area and others. Parents can therefore help children develop their middah of Seder by accustoming them to structure and order. Of course, one should never force this on children; it should be done in a way that is fun and enjoyable.

enjoyable. It is a way to avoid chaos without resorting to punitive or manipulative measures.

It also includes developing certain habits of avoiding aveiros. It is important that both the aspects of Zeriah and Binyan should be cultivated. Without this somewhat robot-like aspect, the child can develop bad habits which are difficult to break later on. By developing a habit to *not* do the aveira, it lowers the nisayon of the Yetzer Hara later in life. The Mishna Berurah's example of this is the habit of speaking lashon hara (OC Siman 343 MB3).

Binyan of a child by aveiros

Not every aveira committed by a child will create a bad habit that one should attempt to prevent children from developing. A habit that is challenging to break is a habit that is done *with* understanding. Children cannot, and therefore do not, create a habit of 'switching on lights on Shabbos' if they are still incapable of understanding *when* Shabbos is and *what* a light switch is. Similarly, children who do not yet understand that there are forms of speech that can hurt others, which is a subtle idea, are not really building a *habit* by speaking lashon hara, the habit of lack of empathy, allowing one to hurt others through speech. Before that level of understanding, the behavior is very weak and easily broken. For such behaviors, parents do not need to intercede, as they do not result in children building habits.

Regarding behaviors which children *will* build a habit for, parents should explain to them, within the child's weak understanding, the idea of *what* the aveira is and *why* we don't do it. This should be done at a younger age than one should explain positive mitzvos to them. Though they will act with less understanding, it is still done with some understanding, and it is important that they should not build that bad habit. Many children at the age of three can understand when Shabbos is and what a light switch is, and they can also understand the basic idea that Hashem created the world and that we rest to celebrate that he did so, and that we don't make changes to Hashem's world on Shabbos. (They do not yet understand the subtleties of why creating a circuit can be a constructive act, but the basic idea of celebrating Hashem creating the world they can understand at that young age). If children forget or are mischievous, one should overlook it, as opposed to admonishing them, which will destroy their self-esteem. When they grow older, they will remember to do it and grow out of their mischievousness. By defining the aveira for them, and explaining to them why we don't do it, without the enforcement of punishment, children will be happy to be able to go along with what you tell them.

There is a downside to getting rid of bad habits in children through the use of reward and punishment. Children will have a much harder time understanding the purpose of refraining from that action later in life. If children act purely based on a habit, they will continue to act that way, without understanding what the reasons for those actions are[16]. In addition, they will think of Torah as a burden, and when they grow older and can make their own choices, they will choose to reject Torah.

The most ideal way to accomplish the Binyan of avoiding the bad habits of aveiros is to take away the challenge. For example, parents can put away muktzeh toys right before Shabbos and take out exciting Shabbos toys. In that way, the challenge of playing with the muktzeh ones has been removed. Another good way is through structure, by making what is beneficial for children to do, fun. Parents should try to find a way to make avoiding a particular bad habit fun[17]. In general, this can be difficult to accomplish. An example of a good idea would be to offer children the job of putting on light switch covers before

---

[16] A habit which is built on understanding will result in a person acting thoughtfully and with meaning and also have the benefit of a habit which makes it easier for one to do an action. A habit built on understanding is good for a person.

[17] Even with their weaker understanding, children will still be acting with some מתוך שלא לשמה intentions [See earlier footnote on מתוך שלא לשמה].

Shabbos, as by involving themselves in 'avoiding the light switches' they will be less likely to play with the switch on Shabbos.

Binyan of a child by positive mitzvos

There is a benefit to having a habit of doing a positive mitzvah as well; however, parents should *not* encourage children for the purpose of developing a habit to do a positive mitzvah. Having a habit of doing a positive mitzvah is not nearly as beneficial as avoiding the formation of a habit of doing an aveira, and there is a negative impact of having the habit.

It is harder to undo an aveira which is a habit than it is to do a mitzvah which a person is not habitual to, when the person understands that they should be doing it.

The very important negative impact one should avoid is causing a person to do [doing mitzvos without thinking [18] מצות אנשים מלומדה

---

[18] There are some mitzvos that are exceptions to this idea, that telling children to do mitzvos before they understand them raises the tremendous concern of them acting with מצות אנשים מלומדה throughout their life.

One of these exceptions may be Negel Vasser. The Mishna Berura explains that tumaah isn't good. One can make it a game; take them out of the crib, fly them to a chair by the sink and quickly wash and done. If they ask why we do it one should answer them, though they won't quite understand, 'To get the tumaah off.' One shouldn't insist that they do it if they really don't like it. If one finds a lenient opinion, they should rely on it as in a situation of *shaas had'chak* [pressing need].

Another example is bringing children into a sukkah; just their presence in the sukkah meaningfully affects them.

A third one is wearing tzitzis. Parents should put tzitzis on their young children if they do not object, and if the child will not ruin the tzitzis.

There are few exceptions.

One should not force these mitzvos, but it is good if one can have children fulfill them.

about their meaning and what significance they have]. That is a very real concern for one who is trained to do mitzvos before they understand their purpose. This is especially relevant to using one's speech, like davening. A whole lifetime of fulfilling that mitzvah can be affected; we have been taught as children to never do mitzvos with *kavanah* [intention] and *havana* [understanding].

The level of maturity for chinuch

Q: If a child can understand that Hashem said we must do a certain mitzvah, but can't understand the reason for the mitzvah, should parents teach that mitzvah with the understanding that 'this is something Hashem said we must do'?
Dr G: In children's understanding, if it is inconvenient for them to fulfill that obligation, then they feel that Hashem is mean; it is hard to do things that we don't want to do. They view parents as messengers of Hashem, making sure that these obligations are fulfilled. The idea of 'Hashem said we have to' is usually invoked to force children to act against the children's wishes.

Q: What if parents just told a child once, and didn't push the child?
Dr G: It doesn't take much to understand the idea of Hashem creating our beautiful world and resting on the seventh day, and the idea that to celebrate that we also don't do constructive activities on the seventh day, like those done in creating the most holy place in the world - the Mishkan.
Parents should use good sense. It is better if children understand a reason for the mitzvah. It is not so simple to understand the idea of 'assur' and be able to follow through on something they were told is

---

This does *not* include saying Modah Ani. Modah Ani is a meaningful recognition and understanding of the gratitude to Hashem for the Neshama being returned to us after it leaves us during the night. One should not take the meaning of this important idea away from children by having them say it before they understand it (see more in **Teaching a child to Speak Nicely**).

'assur' without understanding a reason. Children that are smart enough to understand that 'Hashem said this is assur' are usually smart enough to ask why, and to understand the answer.

In Closing

If parents go to war with children, it solves nothing. One has to be sensible to help children. If they do not have enough self-control, then they are not yet at the age of chinuch. Attempting to force children to fulfill the mitzvos using rewards is not a *mehalech* [acceptable way]. Children can't live in a house where everything is 'No,' where parents always scowl. If children are told too young to not switch on the light on Shabbos, they will often turn on the lights *l'hachis* [to spite] if they do not have a good relationship with their parents. If children do not want to do what they are told they must do, it results in constant negativity. One doesn't always have to *notice* when they see children doing something incorrectly.

Parents have to be careful. If life seems full of demands, and there is pressure attached to mitzvos, it will be harmful to children. To a large extent, the encouraging/forcing is unnecessary in the long run.

Chapter 1

Building Self Esteem
in Young Children

Without being cynical, this chapter should really be labeled "How to not ruin self-esteem in young children."

The first and second years of children's lives are the most important for their self-esteem. Most children are born with a good sense of who they are, but that can be ruined easily. The most important thing is to try to avoid disapproval, while creating structure for children by other means. It is also important to validate children's inherent value, and to help them regulate themselves by being a source of calmness.

What is a 'Child'

It is important to recognize that a child is a human. *Koach habechira* [the ability to choose] for a human is perhaps their most precious possession. It is one of the major aspects of our צלם אלקים. Children are born with good self-esteem; everyone has a sense of their own greatness, their spirituality. Children have feelings. This may be a *chiddush* [novel idea]: Parents should *ask*[19] an older sibling why he or she hit a younger one; there is always a reason. Many tend to view children as primitive computers or robots. Children are not robots that need to be programmed to do what is proper and not to do what is improper. Parents should have expectations for children, but if a child doesn't meet those expectations, it should be dealt with in a loving and educational way. A big part of what is important to children's belief in themselves and to their self-confidence is their ability to regulate their impulsiveness (controlling their impulses when frustrated). When children are in pain, the mother can absorb that pain and conduct herself with calmness. This teaches children to do that for themselves.

They want what they want, and Saying 'No'

When children hit around one year and nine months old, and have a strong sense of koach habechira, that is typically when conflicts begin. The Chovos Halevavos (שער הבטחון פרק ד חלק ד) explains that a person's koach habechira is the ability to choose to try to accomplish something (we are unable to actually accomplish any result). A two-year-old can have very strong feelings; it is their sense of humanity. Children want what they want. They have no idea why *this* choice or this thing is better than *that* choice or that thing. It pays to go along with them when possible. If children's ideas and opinions are addressed, even if they are not agreed with, it is very validating. 'I know you want this, I wish I could get it for you, unfortunately...' Parents should acknowledge their children's *wish* for it.

It is hard for children to distinguish between disapproval of an *action* and disapproval of the *person*. When a parent expresses disapproval of the *way they are acting*, they take it as an attack on *who they are*.

---

[19] If the child is not old enough to express his feelings, it is usually obvious why he hit them.

By the "terrible twos" is when self-esteem is most commonly ruined; children are always doing things that frustrate parents.

Q: Should one always say yes?
Dr G: No. But it pays to be careful before saying 'No.'

Some parents assume the answer is 'Yes.' Some assume the answer is 'No.' It pays to find a way to not have to say no. For parents to naturally want to avoid saying 'no' involves developing the middah of ratzon. Ratzon is described in the Orchos Tzadikkim פרק י״ג and Maalos Hamiddos פרק י׳׳ח: it is the idea that a person wants to fulfill the *retzonos* [wishes] of others. Out of empathy; it hurts them to say no. There are some things which are not necessary for a child, and the child may not want them to happen. In these cases, one should give them leeway. 'Children must wear such and such clothes;' parents should recognize what is really more important.

Sometimes one cannot allow children to have what they desire. Structure is important for children, but it should be implemented without negativity. Child: "I want some cake" Mother: "Have it for dessert; first you have to eat chicken livers" Child: "I want cake." In this scenario, either actual or perceived disapproval frequently comes into the picture. However, if there is a routine in the home then there would be no *hava amina* [possible thought] of a different outcome. In our house candy was never around during the week, and in situations like that there is nothing to desire and therefore no risk of causing parents to express disapproval. [See **Routine and Structure**]

If the cookies are nowhere in sight, and a child asks 'Can I have a cookie' and the mother says 'No' and then says 'Here come play this game with me,' that does not show disapproval.
When it becomes a power struggle is the problem. It's not the fact that the mother said no, it's the forcing.

If the parent's tone is disapproving then it will also affect the children. One study had mothers and children: The mothers were told to say 'yes' and 'no' in both a disapproving tone of voice and an approving tone [ie. both 'yes' and 'no' in an approving way and a disapproving way]. The tone of voice made all the difference.

Sometimes the likelihood of the child perceiving parental disapproval can at least be minimized, by making it a 'memeila' [expected; natural[20]] response. For example, when children start throwing their food then mealtime is over. Parents should perform this as a natural response, without expressing disapproval through language or facial motions. Removing the food should be followed by getting the child involved in another fun activity. This creates a routine that food is only available while it is being eaten and when it isn't being eaten it disappears. It becomes as regular as the sun rising in the morning. It also makes sense to the child. It is likely that there may end up being some disapproval when children protest and say they are still eating, but only if the parent responds in a disapproving way. There may also be some disapproval felt the first couple of times it is implemented, before it becomes routine, but most of the disapproval will be removed.

Once parents have conveyed to children that their feelings are important, and that their parents really love them, it is also beneficial to avoid using the word 'no' itself and even when one is denying the request to do it in a way that doesn't deny them directly. Using the example given earlier in which a child asks for a cookie, instead of saying 'No' (and removing the possibility of sending a message of disapproval by inviting the child to play a game), the mother might just avoid answering 'Yes' or 'No' in the first place, and simply distract the child by asking them to come play a game.

---

[20] Even a response which is expected, but doesn't naturally make sense is good for reducing disapproval. It is even better when the response also makes sense.

Responding to children acting against the parent's wishes – Punishing

Punishment is always an attack on self-esteem. There is the humiliation as well the feeling children have that the parents think that he or she is a bad person.

So often, parents assume a greater degree of intellect in young children, or don't recognize that the concepts they are attempting to convey are actually fairly complex. Children do not understand the difference between "Food is made to be eaten" and "You are bad for throwing food."

I can't understand why parents do 'multiple lectures.' If you tell a child the same thing again at a later time, the child thinks that you think the child is stupid[21]. Children's memories are as good as the memories of adults[22], especially for things that parents made clear that they are a 'bad boy or girl' for if they do or don't behave in a specific way. Parents can tell why a child is acting against the parent's instruction, whether it is because the child forgot, or because the child is being mischievous.

There is a quote from Dr. Twerski that as a child when he did something that wasn't to his father's approval, his father would say "It is *nit pahst*" [it is not befitting for someone of your stature to do an act like that]. For older children, this conveys a respect that boosts their self-esteem about overcoming this nisayon (a four-year-old will not understand this concept).

---

[21] However, see **The Essence of Chinuch** 'Helping a Child access his Seichel' regarding showing children how something they know is also true in a slightly different context. That is different from telling children the same thing again, indicating your belief that the child is stupid. In that case the child didn't understand that the extension was true until you explained it.

[22] One could remind a child, the same way that one would remind one's spouse when it makes sense to [ie. if they have a moment of forgetfulness, and reminding them will provide a benefit in the future to fix what they forgot or to be more careful].

With aversive conditioning [training children to avoid a certain action by making it painful for them when they do the action], children become resentful and it causes antagonism. It is better to stay away from that. That is not to say that negative consequences should never be used[23].

When one disciplines children, it usually comes with anger, and therefore it is not fit to be done. It is hard to identify what triggers us, and how to respond to that trigger in a better way.

Why does a mother lose it when a child colors on the wall, yet again? For some mothers it is *kaas* [anger], that something they care a lot about is being taken from them. With some mothers it is the feeling of being disrespected; 'How dare you do that;' it feels even worse when one is being disrespected. Parents must learn how to deal with their *own* feelings in ways that will not harm their children.

"We don't color on walls" means "I, dictator, say we don't." The child does not have any understanding of why that makes sense. The child thinks "Well, I do want to." If parents insist on forcing children to "bow down" to them, the children will think of their parents as egotists who demand subservience. Avoid accusing children of chutzpah. It is valuable to not be *makpid* [exacting] on your own *kavod* [honor]. To develop kavod for yourself from your children, be a good parent; then they will respect you.

If a child is coloring on the wall, show the child a paper and say "this is where we color." If the child continues to color on the walls, take away what they are using to color and provide the child something else fun to do. Punishing or screaming at the child for ruining your walls will only hurt the child. At a younger age parents should get washable crayons.

Q: What if a child hits a parent?

---

[23] Their proper use is explained below

Dr G: A child won't hit a parent unless the child is very angry and has lost control. Usually there is a reason for that anger. In that situation, punishing the child makes the problem worse. I don't suggest that.

If a child hit a parent out of anger, the first question is 'Why?' Parents should ask their child; children are able to explain themselves. For children who are too young to express themselves, the reason will typically be right on the surface. Usually, the reason is because the parent got angry at the child first. Parents should deal with the situation by addressing the problem, not aggravate the situation more by standing on principle and demanding justice. [See more in **Temper Tantrums**]

Parent's *gaavah* [arrogance] is a very big factor in raising children. If a parent is a big *anav* [humble person] then when that parent punishes it will be out of love, and it will be with a lot of thought for what is best for the child, and the intention that the child should understand the proper way to act in the future. That parent will not punish simply because the child doesn't listen to their orders.

Many aspects of having structure are very important. One shouldn't get the wrong idea and think that parents should 'let the child run the house according to his wishes.' In addition, it is very important to be 'on top of the situation.' A mother should always have the children within striking distance so they can nip issues in the bud, when they are smaller and easier to solve.

Parents should try to find ways to achieve structure, and accomplish goals without disapproval.

Proper use of punishment

When children are old enough, and they understand the idea of why a certain household rule is in place, and also have the self-control to avoid doing that action, then the child can be given a consequence for an incorrect action that the child chose to do. The child chose to fulfill the short-term desire for enjoyment despite knowing that it was an overall harmful thing to do. Receiving a consequence in this case will help the child recognize on a deeper level that the action is harmful and will help the child make the correct choice the next time they are confronted by the challenge of whether to fulfill a short-term enjoyment or avoid long-term harm.

In this case, parents should be very careful to express two valuable messages to their children: they should express that they respect the child's *intelligence* and that they respect the child's *self-control*. Punishing them with the message of 'You are stupid, you are a wild animal' will hurt the child's self-esteem. Parents should also express the message that they love the child and that it hurts them to punish the child, but that they are doing so for the *child's* growth and best interests[24].

Validating a Child's Value

Children don't have an internal monitor to measure themselves as a person, and can therefore be easily affected by positive or negative feedback from others. A great deal of children's self-esteem comes from when they bask in the attention of their caretakers. Attention and approval are very important. Hashem made babies look cute so their parents would properly care for them. Approval, smiling, and noticing when children do unusual things is good for them. Smiling at children is important even when they are very young. Children recognize faces from when they are born, and often respond to smiles. It is especially important to validate them by recognizing what *the children* see as genuine achievements.

---

[24] Household rules which really are not in the child's best interests should not be household rules. However, sometimes rules which protect the parent's interests from being trampled on are also truly in the child's best interest. For example, throwing balls in a living room will break the pictures. For many parents the inability to have pictures in their living room would affect their mood which would affect how they treat their children. Therefore, it benefits those children to have a household rule that balls may not be thrown in the living room.

Looking at a child and smiling is a global message: 'Your essence is wonderful.' Validating achievement gives that message, but it can also put pressure on children to always force themselves to succeed. When children are already happy with their achievement, then joining them in acknowledging it sends a powerful message.

Q: Can a child feel genuinely loved and still have poor self-esteem?
Dr G: If the lack of self-esteem comes from a different source, like from peers or rebbeim, then home might be a refuge. Usually, the lack of love and corresponding lack of self-esteem come from the same source. Showing children you love them feeds good self-esteem. It is *talui zeh bazeh* [dependent on another].
It is much more important that children feel unconditional respect than unconditional love.

Regulation

A big part of children's belief in themselves is that they can regulate their impulsiveness.
It is very important for a mother to be calm when frustrating things happen to her children, and that helps the children deal with their own frustration. Eventually, it leads to self-regulation; children's ability to regulate their own emotions. There was a study done that found that when a mother is calm and relaxed and enjoys holding their baby, then their baby is calm. A tense mother produced a tense baby. Babies respond to their mother's tension by also tensing up. From Day Two[25], a mother's self-regulation can teach a child whose tummy hurts to be calmer, and when that child gets older, *they* will have the capacity to self-regulate.

The calmness of the mother will allow her children to feel uncomfortable feelings and still maintain control. If the child's

---

[25] The day a child comes home from the hospital

discomfort isn't causing the parents to feel uncomfortable, the child will pick up on it and learn to be *soveil* [endure] discomfort. If a mother is calm when children are frustrated, children will learn to handle frustration on their own.

Emotions tend to be contagious. If children are angry or nervous, it tends to create anger or nervousness in the parents. Parents can break this cycle by being calm and empathetic. Any time one is in a contagious situation and the person with them is calm, not only does it help with mood regulation for that situation, the person also learns the skill of being calm despite discomfort. They see that it is possible and attainable.

Even for older children this is important. Whatever children do, parents should not let it make them nervous. If a child breaks a dish, and the parent wants to enforce a consequence, be calm in the response. Calmly say "You're of age, you could have controlled yourself. You were told to not throw baseballs in the living room." If the parents are calm, children will be calm in response, and it will also be a lot more effective. Acting composed also reinforces unconditional love. If, even when parents feel they must punish a child, they are controlled in their temperament, the child will realize that it is coming from a place of genuine concern. If parents act flustered when children go against their wishes, then the punishment comes across as the parent simply reacting in order to protect their own interests.

Nobody is perfect, we do the best we can. If a mother is overtired, and the father is home, it is a good time to bring Daddy into the picture.
It is a good idea to teach babies to nurse from a bottle the day they are born, so the mother is not always needed when the baby cries. At some point the mother will have to return to work, and it will be very hard for the child to learn at that late stage to drink from a bottle. In the meantime, a mother who is always needed to nurse her child can be more cranky towards the entire family, and deprive both the baby and the older children of necessary attention.

If parents are calm, children will see that the world is a trustworthy and peaceful place, and calmness will pervade the household

.

Chapter 2

Holding Children

As much as possible, young children should be held. Research finds that the more children are held during their first two years of life, the more independence they have later in life. It is especially important during the first year of life. 'Children can't have too much holding.' Specifically during feeding, holding has an added *maalah* [advantage]. Feeding is not just nutrition, it shows intimacy and builds attachment between the mother and the baby, which is necessary for the child. One should not 'prop a bottle' as an excuse for a mother not holding their baby.

Psychologist Jean Harlow conducted a study in which infant monkeys were separated from their mothers, and offered either a cold breast made out of wire and wood, but which produced milk, or a warm and furry breast that did not produce milk. The infant monkeys consistently chose the warm and furry breast, which most resembled their mothers, even at the cost of their lives.

When children are held at a very young age, they become secure in their world. This feeling stays with them, and as they get older, they therefore become more secure in themselves and their capabilities. If they are held in their first year, then when they are somewhat older, they will be secure in the knowledge that their mommy is there for them, even if she is not currently visible.

Allowing a baby to cry makes them feel abandoned. Their whole life and sense of security have disappeared. Babies need to be held. Parents should postpone their own activities so that they can care for their children.

Even older children usually want to be held when they are in pain, or in a strange place. It gives them a sense of security. Parents should hold them, and then try to wean them off it. Find them familiar toys, bring familiar foods, or find them a child of similar age to play with.

Q: Until what age does a child need physical contact while drinking a bottle?
Dr G: After one and a half to two years of age, children should not have a bottle/sippy cup[26] anymore. By then they should use a regular cup. Once children are older and drinking from a regular cup at the table or in a high chair, they need to develop independence and one should not hold them during feeding. If a child is using a regular cup during the day, and only using a bottle at naptime or to fall asleep, then *for sure don't* hold them during that bottle, as one wants the child to go to sleep on their own. [See more in **Sleep-training** 'Sleep training specifics and advice'].
Once children aren't interested in being held, one should not force it. That is a good sign; it means they are becoming more independent.

Q: My child likes to be held while I am standing but it is hard. What should I do?
Dr G: Make a compromise. Hold them while sitting down, and if the baby has a tantrum, they will quiet down eventually. The child will learn to be calmed even while being held sitting. Holding a child while sitting is just as beneficial for the child, even though a child prefers to be held standing.

---

[26] [**See Pacifiers during the Day** about the use of sippy cups.]

Children like the motion of standing and walking, but can get used to being held while sitting down. Parents can also use a rocking chair; parents have to compromise between what they are capable of doing and attending to children's desires.

Chapter 3

Giving Attention

Children's need for attention

Children need attention, some more than others.
There are three main reasons that children need attention.

The first reason is to help them build healthy self-esteem [See more in **'Building Self-esteem in Young Children-** Validating a child's value']. The second reason is to help keep them productively occupied. The third is that children should feel that 'their parents are with them.' There is a fourth reason also, to make sure that children don't do things which are damaging to themselves or other children.

For older children, the second need for attention, to help them be productively occupied, means 'always having the child in the corner of my eye.' This attention is needed so that if a child gets bored, you can refocus the child on something fun and interesting. With very little children, attention is needed because 'doing something' means being interacted with by adults. Young children need to be interacted with through being held sometimes, and shown affection. Interaction is what infants 'do.'

For children to feel that 'their parents are with them,' the third need, is both a security need and a comfort need. That feeling is provided by being attentive to the child. As they get older and internalize those feelings of security and comfort, children still need and will ask for attention, but usually not as constantly or consistently. At a certain age they will become even more independent and will not need, or frequently want, their parent's constant attention. However, little children *cannot manage without* their caretaker being on top of them. Even if a mother walks out of the room, children can get scared. "Where is she? When will she be back?" That is part of what hurts children when their mother is on the phone for an indefinite period of time.

Children have to be happy. It is not a mehalech to have a very happy mother and a miserable child.

How much and when

A serious problem is that parents tend not to plan well enough to be able to give their children the proper attention they need. When a mother has a full-time job, and perhaps even brings additional work home, they often cannot give their children the attention they need. Parents must make it a higher priority to give their children necessary attention. Often parents stay up late at night entertaining themselves in various ways and are tired in the morning. They then expect their children to keep themselves busy while they get dressed, instead of the parents waking up earlier to tend to their own needs so that later they will be available to help their children get dressed. Parents need to correct this by having the self-discipline to go to sleep earlier.

Parents should give children the attention they need, even if the children are older. For older children, attention can be in the form of preparation for an activity, such as finding them a friend to play with or something with which they can play. Children who have not yet developed the independence to find playmates or activities on their own need to be helped until they eventually are capable of doing it on their own, until they no longer request it.

Friday afternoons are a common time that children are neglected. Frequently parents are not only preparing for Shabbos, but are also talking on the phone. Parents must plan better to give their children the proper, necessary attention. Parents should do the cooking earlier in the week, or buy food if that isn't an option.

Another common example of when parents neglect to give their children proper attention is when they are on the phone. If a parent is on the phone and a child asks for help, the parent should tell the person on the other end of the phone line to wait, not the other way around.

Q: Don't children have to learn that when Mommy is on the phone they have to wait?
Dr G: No, I don't think so. The child needs a little help. The child is stuck meanwhile, and children don't have a sense of time. Mothers and babysitters are supposed to be available.

Q: When do children learn that they don't get instant gratification?
Dr G: "When they're 18."
The idea of patience is of delaying gratification, essentially controlling desire[27] for a period of time. Children don't have a perspective of time. They are unable to predict how long the period will be and therefore have a very hard time being 'patient.' This is especially hard if parents don't occupy the child during that time. Impulse control develops with age. When children get older they can get into an activity for a longer period of time and the delay is not as painful.

Q: I can sing songs from tapes about patience. Won't that help?

---

[27] Patience is an idea that is dependent on an understanding of time. It is the control of desire, but projected into time. It is controlling a desire for a period of time.

Dr G: Does it work? Pedantic songs aren't bad, but they don't help children.

Personally, I think those songs are good for *me*. They *are* good mussar. I wish I was more perfect.

Q: If I am in the middle of washing dishes, I should stop and help the child?

Dr G: Yes. Turn off the water, dry your hands, help them, and then return to the dishes. Dishes know how to wait; children don't.

Q: If the child wants attention now, should the parents comply *at all costs?*

Dr G: Sometimes you can't.

But there must be a reasonable amount of time that parents give attention to children.

There are very few things more important than taking care of children, and making dinner is almost never one of them. If you are packing a bag for a trip, so you'll leave a little later. If the supper will burn, so take the pot off the stove. Your husband will have to wait for his dinner.

Q: What if I am making dinner for the child, and they want my attention?

Dr G: So what, it will take a little longer to finish preparing dinner.

Parents need to refocus the child, and then they can continue with their dinner prep.

Children don't need constant attention to feel that their parents are attentive, as long as they have what to do.

Learning to delay gratification is *prishus* [abstention from worldly pleasure]. As children get older and have a longer time perspective, they do learn to be patient with adults when the adult can't easily be interrupted, and they are able to entertain themselves with other things before their needs are served.

"You can't teach a child to be considerate by showing disapproval when a child is inconsiderate." Being considerate is an *inyan* [aspect of] of chesed. You can't expect anything like that from a child under three (or even somewhat above three). It is not an effective way to teach consideration.

Giving attention while doing other things

It is hard to get anything done when one has little children. A distinguished mother of a bunch of little children was asked: "When do you get anything done?" Her reply was "When they're asleep."

Children should be kept busy, and mothers should be in a position to help children when needed. She should always keep the child in the corner of her eye, and be in a position to refocus the child on the activity at hand, or find the child a new dimension of the activity if they lose focus. If the mother is able to do that, then she can be doing other things also.

As long as children come first, parents can multitask; they can roll a ball back and forth to the child while talking on their bluetooth. This is assuming that the parent will attend to the child if requested, and that the person on the phone is cooperative. For very little children, parents can get a carrier so they are holding them while doing other things. Babies can be put in a bouncer. They gain more from non-electric ones where they can play with the toys, instead of just pressing a button and being entertained. The child is doing something active. Parents can sometimes involve children in their adult task so that they can take care of it without neglecting the child[28].

It's very hard when there are also older children in the family, to be there for all of the children simultaneously. Sometimes older children

---

[28] This has other benefits as well, as discussed in **Essence of Chinuch** and **Children Helping in the House**.

get too little attention (especially if the little one is cute). Sometimes the younger one cries and gets attention and the older one remembers forever that they are not worth much[29]. Sometimes children need attention to solve a problem between siblings[30].

Occupying a young child

With little children, 'doing something' is getting interacted with by adults.

Q: For a one-year-old who has been held for a long time, if one is not trying to get them to go to sleep, which is better, a Rocker or a Pacifier?
Dr G: They should play with toys.
Children are very inventive.
Even young children are. They love pots and pans.

Q: What about a three-month-old?
Dr G: They can be in a car seat watching what the mother is doing.

When one must attend to one's own needs

If a person understands what is going on inside of themselves, they will have a proper perspective. If the food is burning, it is understandable why a parent has to take care of the food. It also depends on what the child is demanding. If a child asks 'sit down and play a game' it is different from 'I can't put this puzzle piece in.' Sometimes the best thing is distraction; 'I really have to finish this thing, I can't sit down with you, but here's something you can do by

---

[29] See **Caring for a Child with a Newborn Sibling**

[30] See **Dealing with Multiple Children**

yourself.' It is a big *b'dieved*[31] [course of action when an incorrect thing was done prior] to not be able to give children proper attention.

If a child interrupts a parent's conversation with a relative, let him. If the child just wants to say something quickly, it is okay. If he wants to take the parent out of the conversation, it is a different story.

In summation: I am objecting to the rationalization by parents of 'I am doing the child a favor' and 'teaching them patience' by forcing them to wait for various reasons. Parents should, however, understand that sometimes the parent's needs *do* come before the child's needs. However, it is not a *stirah* [a contradiction] to appreciate the needs of the child.

[In our dear chaver R' Ezzie's words: "I may not be Dr. Goldman but I'm trying to be" is the proper perspective].

---

[31] Parents should avoid these situations by preparing better beforehand.

Chapter 4

Emotional Validation

It is important that parents validate their children's emotions. This plays a role both in helping them have proper self-esteem and in helping them recognize and validate their own emotions.

Helping children have proper self-esteem

It is important that parents *not* perceive children as acting *bad* in any given situation, but rather recognize what the child's feelings and reasonings are. Children act because of reason, though their reasons are different from adults. They feel their reasons are right. Sometimes what they are doing is in fact incorrect, but they are *not malicious*. If children get the sense that parents think that what they are doing is *bad*, they will feel rejected and humiliated. Even if parents can't go along with or condone the child's actions in a particular situation, children should at least feel that their parents understand the thought processes that led them to take that action.

Children cannot understand why they can't have more dessert or can't have longer to play. It is important for parents to speak to them and validate them. Let them know that you understand that they would like to, but unfortunately they can't right now (and of course, that you have something wonderful waiting for them as an alternative).

This helps develop children's sense of self-esteem and their ability to validate themselves. By doing so, parents are recognizing that children are human, and that their opinion is valid, appreciated, and worthy of taking into account. Even more than unconditional love, children need unconditional respect.

Parents should notice their children's emotions and acknowledge them; this is validation. 'I see that you feel hurt,' 'You must be angry, what happened?' 'What's wrong? You look sad.'

When children feel that they have gotten hurt, a parent should validate that the child is hurt. No pain is too small to put a bandaid on, give them a kiss, and send them out to play. Parents should not, however, validate a minor pain too dramatically, to the extent that the child stops playing and sits on the parent's lap. Yet even when a child has only a slight pain[32] a parent should recognize and validate the child for their feeling that they are experiencing pain.

Q: I feel that sometimes my child is *manipulating* me to give them a bandaid, and really they are not very hurt.
Dr G: Manipulation is trying to *force* a parent to go *against their better judgment*. Getting a bandaid and some validation isn't manipulation.
If, however a child is entirely pretending to be hurt, maybe something is in fact wrong. Parents should then ask themselves 'Why do they have to go to such an extreme length to get attention?'

---

[32] Sometimes children come without claiming any injury, they come just because they need a little attention. If the child is 'asking for attention,' give the child a little attention; then send the child out to play. There is nothing wrong with needing a little attention. The child can run out to play, run back to Mommy and make sure that she's still there for them, and then run back away to play. It is good to give them that little reassurance and validation. [see 'Giving Attention']

Q: Maybe validating children with bandaids isn't so good; then they will always need a bandaid, and parents might not have one available. Maybe a hug, which is always available, is better.

Dr G: Giving a hug *and* a bandaid is better.

A bandaid addresses a child's feeling of pain more directly. The child thinks they are hurt, a bandaid addresses and validates that. It is a good idea to bring bandaids with you so children will feel that their parents are there for them.

Helping a child recognize their emotions

Another important reason to validate children's emotions is in order to help them learn to recognize and properly identify their own emotional states. Young children need to learn to label their emotions. With children who cannot describe what they are feeling, a parent must try to figure out what the child is feeling and then the parent must put it into words.

Chapter 5

Routine and Structure

Importance of having routines

It is good for children to have certain normal household routines; it gives them a sense of structure. Children are black and white in this way[33], they are used to routine. Routine helps avoid the negativity from children not wanting to do things which are necessary for their own well-being.

It is important to implement and keep routines running in positive ways. The best way to implement routines is through fun; children will look forward to all elements of the routine; each piece of it is fun. If a routine is implemented with force and negativity, children will respond in kind.

For example, eating can be followed by playing, and parents can say 'Let's quickly eat so we can go play!' Children frequently look forward to bedtime. They get to see their father, they play a little, he sings a

---

[33] Children can understand sensible distinctions, like only having candy at certain times. They don't work well with parents capitulating sometimes and at other times not, depending on how generous the parent is feeling or on how much strength they have to fight with the child.

song and reads a chapter from a book. For eating, one can say 'Come eat and we'll talk about baseball.' One could also say 'Quickly get dressed and then Mommy will have time to prepare a yummy food' (not as a reward, rather it will provide her the time).

One must have flexibility with time. Parents must expect that children will take extra time to complete nearly all tasks.
'I don't like that shirt, I want the other shirt.' Parents should get up early so they can spend time with their children in the morning, taking care of their needs, instead of the parents using the time to take care of their own needs.

Mealtime routine

Lunch is at lunchtime; if children don't eat, they will have to wait for the next meal. If they skip a meal and are hungry, they will realize that they should eat when food is served, otherwise they will have to wait for the next meal. A meal or snack should be served at intervals of about 3 hours (breakfast, snack, lunch).

Q: Is it important for them to have this structure? If it works for me, can I give them a second lunch?
Dr G: There are two reasons for set mealtimes. The first reason is that it is inconvenient for the parents to always serve food. The second reason for why it is important to have structured meals is so that children won't be like the Klal Yisrael in the Midbar: 'chickens pecking in the garbage,' always nibbling. Children who eat like that when they are young will develop negative food habits with long term effects. [See 'Zeriah U'Binyan']

There are multiple problems with always nibbling. If children are eating all morning, they probably won't be eating healthy foods, and it is more likely that they will be eating snacks. In addition, nibbling causes a certain addiction. Parents frequently have this problem. They are constantly nibbling when they are stressed. It is not good for their weight, and it is not good for their attitude toward food. Food is eaten for health, it is eaten to serve Hashem; it should not be used as a cure for stress. If it is being used to escape one's challenges, it will mask growing problems instead of allowing one to deal with them.

Q: Is it okay for children to do other things while eating, like playing, or listening to or reading books?
Dr G: Often, that will cause meals to last forever.
It turns into an occasion where children get a lot of attention. They get involved in the game and forget to eat their pizza. It is better to say 'The table is just for eating, during mealtime. You can leave whenever you want, but once you leave you are done. But, I advise you to finish your pizza.' You can also add "Finish quickly and we'll be able to play together!"

Q: Should one let their child play during meals if that is the only way to get them to eat?
Dr G: If it is the *only* way to get them to eat. Parents have to be inventive to ensure that their child's wellbeing is adequately taken care of. My mother used to bribe me with a fun activity so I would eat a food which I hated but she thought was very important for me, beef liver (smothered in ketchup). Something which the child needs, one has to figure out a way to get it done.

Q: If a father doesn't have other time to spend with his children, should he play with them during supper?
Dr G: If that's the only way to spend time with them.
It is better to get supper done first. The best thing would be that supper was done *before* the father gets home, and then he can play with them when he gets home.

Chapter 6

Babysitters and Playgroups

Subbing for a mother

Choosing a babysitter is a very big responsibility. Ideally, children need a mother. Sending a mother out to work shows the value of learning, but it has to be justified by finding a suitable substitute for Mother.

What is needed is a person who loves children. A lady who has feelings like a mother does, and is always running to help the baby. One must find a woman with compassion and *mesiras nefesh* [self-sacrifice]. Sometimes it is difficult to find a person like that; babysitters typically work for the money.

Observe what happens when the babysitter first comes in. If she says "Oooh, how cute,' it is a good sign. If she walks over to the parents and says 'How much do you pay,' it is a bad sign.

In general, if the woman is younger it is better. Younger women usually have more energy, and an instinctive interest in children. An older woman who is desperate for money is usually not as good. In addition, the societal upbringing of babysitters from some countries is both rough and self-centered.

It could take a couple of days to find a babysitter. Don't forget, these are your children. The babysitter will spend a large part of the day, for most of the week, with your children. She needs to fit the 'standards for a mother.'

Children's needs

A lot depends on the age of the child.

Babies need to be held, and held calmly. Babies need to be nurtured when they are not feeling well, and responded to promptly when they call for attention.

A two-year-old needs to try out how the world works, and has an increased need to be creative and to manipulate things. For language skills, children need to talk to an adult that is adept in the child's language. The best thing for a two-year-old child is to have a babysitter who is young and interested in children, who will get down on the floor with them, and who plays interactively. A 'lady on her cell phone' might be okay for little infants if she is holding them and giving them attention by way of being held, but that will not work for two-year-olds.

Multiple children

It is a problem when one feels the *need* to share a babysitter.

A common question is 'Can a newborn share a babysitter with another newborn and a two-year-old?' Some babysitters can handle it, some cannot. Some mothers can handle it and some cannot. The rule of thumb is that if a mother couldn't do it, a babysitter certainly can't.

Parents must have confidence that the babysitter can manage what they are being given.

Generally, it is easier to have a two- or three-year-old and one baby. An older child is more independent and their needs are different, so a person can more easily care for both of them.

Having two two-year-olds sometimes doesn't work. Sometimes one or both are aggressive and the babysitter is constantly breaking up fights.

Playgroups

The biggest question in babysitting is 'Should I put a two-year-old in a group or use a babysitter?'

It depends on their needs, but in general two-year-olds do not play well together, except perhaps under very tight supervision. At that age there is not very much of a *maaleh* [advantage] in interacting with other children. Sometimes a child is happy to have other children around even if the child is not playing with them. Sometimes one of the children bullies the others.

Three-year-olds can play cooperative games, they can participate in group activities. But at the age of two, children need a babysitter. Either one, two, or three children who share a babysitter. The ideal is to find a couple of children who don't tear each other apart. The parents can share some of the costs, while ensuring that their children still receive individualized attention.

Playgroups have the problem of children not getting along with each other, but multiplied. For seven children to have one caretaker can easily deteriorate into the Morah spending the whole time changing diapers and breaking up fights. This is not to say that every two-year-old group is *assur* [forbidden], but one has to look very carefully into them. I shudder to think of the effect on the next generation due to mass-production playgroups.

For a three-year-old, there begins to be a maaleh of interaction. One can see in each child when they are happy to play with others. One can judge a child's maturity when they are ready to apply for a playgroup, and see if the child will be on par when the year starts. Even if the child only turns three in November, most of that year the child will be three and can be in a playgroup.

At three years of age, children begin to develop the skills of cooperation and competition, a sense of doing things together. This should be done under careful supervision. A playgroup can have play-centers, which are carefully structured. The children should be taught, in order to guide them in using the play-centers. They can choose a project, and are shown how to do it. They can be guided in cooperation: 'You do the head, you do the tail.' Children learn cooperative games, and they learn competitive games.

It is a negative when children bring home projects that are mostly the work of the teacher and some blotching of paint by the child. Another negative for two-year-olds is when the Morah makes them sit in a circle. I sadly hear all the time "What should I do? The Morah says my child needs to be evaluated. He runs around during circle time." That is normal behavior for children.

There must be sufficient staff to care for the children. Over six children per staff member is typically illegal. Five or six children per staff member is bad, but could be acceptable. Four children is really better. A playgroup with a ratio of eight children to one staff member is ridiculous, it is a cow herd.

Q: What are the exceptions for when one should use a drop-off?
Dr G: The alternative to using an unacceptable drop-off should be to drop yourself off at home to care for your child! Children must be cared for properly.

Getting a Jewish babysitter

I can't say it's *not* important to have a babysitter who is Jewish. The Rosh Yeshiva zt"l said having a babysitter who is Jewish is a maaleh, as they naturally have the middah of rachmanus. However it is not the first, second, or even third priority. If one has the choice of a young woman who will play on the floor with the children and make them happy, or an older lady, often an immigrant, who is in it for the money and spends the time on her phone, then obviously the younger lady is better. There is no need to worry, she won't teach her religion to your little child.

I am afraid a lot of the attitude against this comes from a built-in prejudice towards gentiles. It is a sad thing. The Alter [of Slobodka] says we can't fathom the level of *Tzelem Elokim* [resemblance of G-d] in non-jews, and certainly a Jew. Whatever they do with their life, they have a Tzelem Elokim and it may come out in very good ways. It is true that deep down, Jews are 'Rachmanim, baishanim,' and even though sometimes it doesn't show, it is *built into* a Jewish person. However, if a different lady, despite not being Jewish, expresses slightly more compassion, one should choose her.

Q: What about the rule of 'Eisav soneh l'Yaakov'?
Dr G: It *could* come out, but it doesn't always.
Rus came from outside Yisrael; some non-jews are exceptional. Perhaps deep down they have that hatred, but they express compassion. In some Jews, the rachamim doesn't come out at all. They hate the job they are doing.

Dealing with your babysitter

Mothers sometimes micromanage babysitters. There is more than one way to be loving and caring. One must remember, a babysitter is also a human. She has her own *daas* [way of thinking], and her own philosophy of doing things.

Being on the phone a lot is not a different philosophy, that's you paying and her not working. You want her to be interacting with the children. Children need attention, some more than others. Attention means 'always having the child in the corner of my eye.' If the child gets bored, the child needs to be refocused on something fun and interesting. It means telling the person on the other end of the phone line to wait. The child needs a little help. Meanwhile the child is stuck, children don't have a sense of delay.
Mothers and babysitters are supposed to be available.

Q: If you see the babysitter on the phone more than you like, nothing crazy but more than your wife would, what should you do?
Dr G: If you are not thrilled, then keep her for now and look for better for next year. You can try to speak with her. Some babysitters are interested in advice. Some are like a tzadeikes and will take rebuke. Give the babysitter leeway in having her own style, but being on the phone too much is not 'a different approach.'

Being a somewhat imperfect babysitter is understandable. It is difficult for the child's *mother* to do the whole Sunday! A good babysitter can sometimes do a better job than mothers; their parnassah depends on it. R' Reuven Feinstein is quoted as saying, 'By Moshe, Yocheved was paid to take care of him. This is how you get a Moshe Rabbeinu.'

Q: The babysitter is doing everything fine, but she isn't warm, she is more business-like. Is that okay?
Dr G: It is worse if she is warm and fuzzy but not doing what she is supposed to be doing. It depends on if the child likes her or not. If you say 'we're going to Mrs. So-and-So' and the child says 'I don't want to go,' it is a good indication that the child doesn't like her. Is the child happy when they are with the babysitter? Even if she is not warm, the child may still perceive love through the feeling that 'I know she cares about me because she takes care of me.' If she is also warm it is

even better. If she is gruff it depends; if it is attacking the child's self-esteem it is no good.

It is a good idea to be generous in paying babysitters. It is a *very* good idea when you consider that she is taking care of your child. If you pay them better, they will take better care of your child.

When to fire a babysitter

When to fire a babysitter is a hard question to answer. The rule of thumb is that if a woman would excuse *herself* for doing the behavior in question once in a while, then parents should also be okay with the babysitter doing it once in a while.

Mothers get distracted on the phone once in a while, they scream at children once in a while. There are many things mothers do on single occasions which they don't do regularly. If the babysitter is basically doing what she should (she is attached to the children, she sits on the floor with them, she keeps them busy), but once in a while she gets frustrated, that is not a reason to fire her. Even if she hits the children once in a while, it is not necessarily a reason to fire her.

If she sits on the couch a large part of the time, and she is on the phone a large part of the time, that isn't 'not quite as good,' and it *is* a reason to fire her. Leaving a child in the stroller in the park and talking to her friends *is* a good reason to fire a babysitter.

Q: Doesn't a person have to have red lines (ie. no leeway for things the parent has told the babysitter she may not do)?

Dr G: There is one thing you have to know: people are people.

If a person had a 'violation of trust' red-line, they would be supervising their spouse in the kitchen every night. If you see your spouse do something that isn't *lechatchila* [the completely proper way to act] but he/she must have just forgotten, don't say anything. A babysitter is also a person, and therefore will sometimes make mistakes, even about things she understands are important to be careful about. It depends how serious it is.

Q: What if the babysitter took the baby home?

Dr G: That is a bigger deal. It depends on how much you trust her, and how long she has been with you.

Of course you should have red lines. But be flexible about it. For the most part, a babysitter taking a child to her house is a big no-no. If it happened once, she might just need a big reprimand, or she may need to be fired

Chapter 7

Preparing a Child for a New Baby

At a certain age, children will notice any changes in the mother. If they ask about the changes, parents should explain to them about the baby that will be arriving. One should answer a question which is asked, but one doesn't have to answer a question that isn't yet asked. Children won't feel that something was hidden from them, as it was explained to them as soon as they noticed anything (and of course they ask if they notice something).

The reasons that one should tell children about the future addition to the family is both to get the child excited, and to avoid surprising them. If the child hasn't asked yet, parents should inform them at least three to four weeks before the baby is due that the mother is expecting a child. One should make a judgment based on the mother if there is a reasonable possibility that she may give birth early. The other reason to tell children a couple weeks in advance is to get them excited. It is important to get children excited about having a new baby. There is no need to tell children earlier than that, as it is an uncomfortable thing for them, because they are concerned about the baby's competition for what they have.

R' Wolbe says that parents should help a child look at the situation as 'We are having a baby.' Parents should get children very excited about the new addition to their family. To whatever extent children can participate in helping the new baby, they will feel that the baby is 'theirs.' Parents should place the baby on the child's lap and teach them how to give the baby a bottle without being rough on the baby. One should not let them run around with the baby. Sometimes children can help with the baby only on mommy's lap. In general babies are more resilient than one thinks, and one should not be overly cautious about allowing children to help with the baby. Of course if one sees that an older child has evil intentions, one must protect the baby, preferably by distracting the older child into something else fun.

Depending on their age, sometimes the best way to prepare a little girl is to give her a dolly of her own even before the baby is born. It helps them understand what a baby is and how to care for them, and helps them get excited.

One should also let children know in advance that there is a special place for mommies to have babies when Hashem makes the baby come out of mommy's tummy. Mommy will go there when it is the special time and [tell them who[34]] will take care of you, and then mommy will come home with our baby! One shouldn't tell children about disappearing to the hospital too soon, as it is a traumatizing piece of information. But one should make sure that children know beforehand. A week and a half or two weeks is usually enough time, but it can depend on the mother.

For children who can't keep track of what day of the month it is, there is another reason to avoid telling them too early about a new baby[35]. Because children don't have a time perspective, they are constantly

---

[34] It is important that parents tell children who will be taking care of them when parents inform them that there will be a time when they will go to the hospital. In addition, it should be a person who the child is comfortable and familiar with.

[35] Or anything else, even very exciting things like weddings.

wondering when the awaited event will occur, and it is uncomfortable for them having no idea when in the future it will happen.

Chapter 8

Caring for a Child with a Newborn Sibling

It can be a big problem for children when another baby is born into the family. It is easier when the older child wasn't the only child; then the older child was always sharing the attention of their parents, but it can still be a problem. A first-born child[36] has the biggest problem. They were the center of the world, and then all of a sudden, their mother sneaks off and comes back with their competition.

A lot depends on the wisdom of the mother. The absolutely worst thing to do is to take the baby into a bedroom and close the door. This is a clear indication to the older child that they are now worth nothing, or are at least a poor second.

It is better that the mother has help to take care of the baby. If there are two children, it is better that the mother takes care of the older child herself, while the person helping cares for the baby.

---

[36] When the first-born child is young in age it is the hardest (this is the same for any 'older' child; the younger in age they are, the harder it is). When the first-born is a bit older, they are able to understand the situation more, and the new baby is not competing with them for their toys and friends.

The needs of a baby are very different from those of a toddler. Usually, the needs of both can be handled at once. If they can't be, usually *the baby* can wait. The baby will scream, but after they get what they need, they will not remember the delay. The three-year-old, however, will remember.

For nursing mothers, there is no inyan of tznius in front of a three-year-old. No matter the older children's ages, a mother is able to use a nursing cover, and she should allow the older children to be with her and not shut them out. The mother should nurse and also read a book to the toddler, thereby giving attention to both of them. A three-year-old who is made to wait will remember forever.

The effect on a newborn to be made to wait

Q: Does the newborn feel neglected that they are made to wait?
Dr G: The newborn will forget it. Babies cry. It shouldn't happen too often, but it happens somewhat. A newborn doesn't have too much memory. It is not such a big deal, if it doesn't happen twenty-five times a day.

Consistent neglect is very harmful. The baby feels emptiness, their needs are not being cared for, they call out and there is no mother to nurture them. Every baby needs a mother to be there for them. Even though a baby will not remember the incidents of neglect, if repeated often they will create a feeling which *will* stay with them. However, neglect for a few minutes, while the older child's needs are met in order to convey to the older child that they are important, will not harm the newborn.

A mother's first focus must be on her children, but there will be times that she cannot take care of *all* of their needs *immediately*. For a mother with a couple of children, her goal is to keep the older children busy, and she cannot always be nurturing the baby. Sometimes temporary neglect is acceptable, if there is sufficient enough of a need[37].

The effect on a toddler to be made to wait for a different child

Keeping children waiting every once in a while is not such a problem. It depends on what the mother is doing. It is often a good strategy to cater to the needs of the three-year-old if their needs only take a moment. If you can't, then you can't. If the mother is consistently taking care of the baby when they need attention, and ignoring the older children, the children will pick up on that.

The three-year-old will develop a jealousy towards the one-year-old, and this feeling can persist into adulthood. It is not good for the sibling relationship, and it is not good for the parents, as it can cause fighting between the siblings. The feeling comes as a result of resentment towards the baby for *existing*, and also towards the mother for bringing the baby into existence. The three-year-old will do things that annoy the parents. The negative response of the parents to this can create a cyclical response pattern that worsens the situation, as the child will be resentful due to that negativity as well. There can be a lot of bitterness and power struggles.

The effect on a toddler who is neglected in favor of a baby is worse than that of neglecting a toddler in favor of one's work. It has all the same disadvantages, plus the comparison to the younger sibling. With neglect in favor of a baby, children get the impression that the mother

---

[37] Preparing simple food for dinner is a basic need for which a person can understandably divert attention from a child. One who wishes to prepare a seven-course dinner, even if they would be embarrassed without that level of extravagance, should find a different way to be able to prepare it, without compromising on their children's welfare. In general, it depends on the level to which parents are able to forgo physical pleasures in order to provide for children in the ideal way.

hates them. Children feel unloved when parents spend a significant amount of time with a sibling instead of them.

Two- and three-year-olds remember a lot. Even if they do not remember specific events, they remember their general feelings about how things went. Children run lovingly to their parents who take care of them. If they are told to 'go away,' that has a very big impact. If the parents say 'go away' and then give attention to the baby it is even worse.

Chapter 9

Dealing with Multiple Children: Fighting and Sharing

Children Fighting

The most important thing to do when children are fighting is to understand *why* each child is motivated to make an issue, enough to provoke a fight.

Identifying the Problem

Sometimes, if children are old enough, parents can sit down and talk with them. 'You have what is more appropriate for your age. Why are you always taking what the little one has?' Sometimes you will get a clear answer; even if they are too young to express it in conversation, they still express it somehow. Once the child conveys what his or her reasons are, parents can help find a solution that works for both of them.

For older children, it is helpful simply so the child is *aware* of what is causing the challenge, so that after changes are made the parent can point out to the child that negativity may no longer be warranted. It can also help in finding the child activities which they are happy to do together.

Some children always seem to want 'the toy that the other child has.' The issue isn't the toy, it is *sinaah* [hatred] or jealousy of the other child. It can also be a way of provoking the mother, sometimes because the child feels neglected or treated unfairly by the mother. Parents must know what the problem is.

Sometimes the babysitter is involved. There may be two children who are the same age, and one child is resentful; either that there is a babysitter, or that they are not getting the full attention of their caretaker. If they don't like the babysitter, then they will be cranky and likely to start fights.

Often fighting with another child becomes a power-struggle between a child and a caretaker. One child gets reprimanded or punished for hurting the other one, and then the child is angry and wants to get back at the other. Then it continues in a circle.

Not every pair of children get along.

Finding solutions

Very frequently, the cause of children fighting is a lack of attention. Sometimes they fight to get attention. In addition, when children are unsupervised, and not kept busy and happy, they tend to bother people. When they are given the attention they were lacking, the problem will disappear. If a mother has limited time in-between coming home from work and when the children are in bed, a good strategy is that Bubby shouldn't call at that time, or if she does, the mother shouldn't answer the phone, and instead remain focused on giving her children all available attention. [see '**Giving Attention**']

If a child is jealous of the attention given to a sibling, parents can solve this problem by providing increased, proper attention to the child who was not being given enough. If a child is jealous of a sibling's talents, parents should build up that child's talents in areas in which he or she has strengths.

Sometimes it is because the child is being rushed from one task to another, instead of being brought from one to the other in a loving and relaxed manner. The child is uncomfortable and that leads to fighting. Parents should utilize routines with positive anticipation and children will not be uncomfortable

Sometimes children don't like other children. This might be because a child is being bullied by another child, or because the other child is being loud or disturbing the child. If it is bullying, parents should identify if the bullying is occurring because the other child is prone to bullying and if the child in question is prone to *being* bullied. Children frequently bully if they are being treated incorrectly in other areas of their day; they take out their frustration on other children. It can come from issues with siblings, other children, or because the child is jealous that their parents are spending time with their younger siblings. Correcting those areas of mistreatment will usually solve the drive to bully. Some children are particularly prone to being bullied if they are timid, anxious, and easily burst into tears. Unfortunately, other children find it fun and easy to bully such children. Parents should strengthen the bullied child's sense of self. This will both help the child stand up for themselves, and will also reduce the degree to which they are bothered by being attacked. When the child is harder to bully and their reaction is less fun the bullying will usually cease.

Everyone wants to be the first to get anything. Children do well with black and white rules[38]. They do *not* do well with things being

---

[38] Sometimes a good rule can be that something always starts with the oldest, explaining that the Torah gives kavod to a *bechor* [first-born], like a kohen, or

predicated on the seemingly 'arbitrary' decisions of parents, primarily decided based on how the parents are feeling at the time.

Sometimes two children just don't get along with each other. One of the worst errors in this type of situation is the common case where a mother will suggest to another mother that she can come visit and that their children who are the same age will play while the mothers talk. Likely the mothers disregard both children, and the child whose home it is (like a two-year-old) feels that a strange child has come and is taking their toys, and protests "They are my toys!"
A good idea in this situation is for the visitor to bring toys from their own home with them, and then if the child whose home it is, is being possessive, the visiting child can play with their own toys.
In all situations, parents must keep their child in the corner of their eye to avoid problems.

Q: Is it common for one to visit another person and bring their own toys?
Dr G: No, it is not common for one to bring their own toys, but it is common that children make a ruckus.
Sometimes it is even easier if they meet in the park instead of one of their homes.

---

something similar. (Younger children may not understand it at all at the time, but when they get older they can appreciate it. However, it isn't the full reason for doing it that way.) In addition, for children too young to understand an explanation, if parents always use one system, then they will assume that it is 'the way it is,' and simply accept it. This can be useful for where children sit at the table. If the seats are always that way, and you keep it consistent, then they will understand that it will be how it is, and will accept it. Parents can do seating other ways if they want to be more flexible, but it can lead to fighting whenever the routine is broken. Where there is a possibility of *machlokes* [argument], this can be a solution. Though younger children suffer a slight discomfort of not getting things first, it will reduce the discomfort of fighting, and they will be happier in the end. Having a set rule also which aligns with the easiest way to complete the process (as opposed to something more arbitrary like starting at the oldest) it is even better as it will result in fewer complaints and less discomfort to children. Whatever works for the family is good.

Q: Is it a good solution that if children are fighting over something, Daddy takes the item and puts it away, so that neither will play with it? Each of them is happy that the other one doesn't have it.

Dr G: That is okay, if it is not accessible and not visible anymore. They will play with something else now. Maybe they will learn a lesson, maybe they won't. Probably they won't, but now there is peace. If there is an unhealthy dynamic evolving, parents have to address it; if it is a one-time thing, this can be a solution. If it is constant, either between children or between parent and child, then the parents must address the problem.

Children bothering each other

Give each child what will make them happy. For very small children, little things excite them. When a baby is bothering an older child, entertain and distract the baby.

Q: What should I do when my older child is playing with blocks, and my younger child is knocking them down?

Dr G: Keep each child involved in an activity appropriate for them. Little children have shorter attention spans. They need more interaction to keep them involved, and new ideas on how to play with what they have.

Q: Can I teach my four-year-old to put blocks up for the baby so the baby won't bother them?

Dr G: Sometimes this means that the mother is not giving attention to either one. Distracting and entertaining a baby takes wisdom, consideration, and love. To take responsibility for a baby's happiness is expecting more than usually exists in a four-year-old.

Q: How should one deal with boredom? My child bothers their sibling since they are 'bored.'

Dr G: Putting toys in front of children may not be sufficient

The toy *was* interesting, but now the child needs another person, or to learn new ways to play with the same toy. They may need the companionship of other people.

Now more than the previous generation, children need to be entertained. I'm not sure why. Perhaps it is because children are more damaged in their self-esteem by their parents, and need to be validated more. Perhaps it is because mothers are not at home as much.

Children get involved in bothering others when they don't have action happening to keep them occupied. Sometimes it is best to have the older child play on the table, or to put up a *mechitzah* [divider] between them so that the baby won't bother the older child. The younger child will scream (alerting you that they need attention to be occupied), but they won't bother the older chilren.

Sharing

Children think 'what I want is mine.' It takes a while until they understand the idea that objects can belong to other people. Even adults have a hard time with the idea[39].

Sometimes it helps to buy two of an item, so that children won't fight over it; however that doesn't always solve the problem. Sometimes a child wants *both*. In such a situation, parents should try to figure out why that is. Perhaps the child wants to get the parents angry, to push their buttons, or to get back at them for something. It is good to figure out what is behind the child's behavior.

---

[39] There is a story with the Shach: He took a man to a din Torah in front of another gadol, and presented a complicated argument. The gadol said to the Shach, 'I would have agreed with you, but I saw the opposite opinion in the new sefer 'Sifsei Cohen' [The Shach's sefer].' We see how hard it is for humans to view what doesn't belong to them in an objective light.

Sometimes parents can find a game that children can play together (with supervision).

Parents can give two- and three-year-olds separate things to entertain them, with reasonable separation.

It is not a good idea to 'take turns' playing with an object. Children have no sense of time, and are resentful when 'the time is over.' However, if one has to enforce turns, they have to. It is usually a battle when the time for 'exchange' comes, even if one uses a timer. Until they reach a certain age, children have no sense of time.

Better than a time-based interval exchange is when the designation for the toy to be exchanged is measured through an achievement-based measure. For example 'After you finish building a tower, it is your brother's turn to use the blocks.' Parents do not want a war when exchanging activities. Sometimes it is better to have separate or coordinated activities.

Whatever works happily is good.

Chapter 10

Children with Different Opportunities

Learning to endure suffering is *not* something parents must teach children.

Hashem provides suffering for all of us, much more than we would provide for ourselves.

Parents don't have to provide more.

When parents can limit the pain of one child not getting what another child is getting, that is great. When they can't, they can't (and the child will learn that their parent cannot always provide them with whatever they want). In general, the expense is not very great. Suffering will occur, and tantrums will occur, but parents must do their best to be kind.

If an older child is going to Six Flags, and the younger child is not yet old enough to go on the rides, bring the younger child to a special park also. Sometimes a younger child is taken to a place suitable only for younger children; so give the older child something else.

If an older child is getting a candy, a younger child could usually also have something compensatory. Even things that seem small to adults are very meaningful to children, and it pains them to see others getting what they aren't.

Sometimes it is a good idea to avoid the situation occurring *in front* of the child. Try to avoid them seeing the other child get what they can't have. When you can, it is good for parents to do that, to keep a sense of fairness.

If a child gets a reward for accomplishing something, then the other child may not necessarily need to be given something. They can understand that when they accomplish goals they also 'earn' and get rewarded.

If a teacher gives their class something, and the sibling wasn't treated that way by *their* teacher, then it is appropriate to give them something. The child thinking that 'the school I'm sent to is unfair' is better to avoid. Sometimes that child will get something from their teacher, which their sibling does not get, and that can be pointed out. If they are both being given a special treat, but separated by a period of time, the child may not be able to see past the gap in time and will feel unfairly treated. It depends on the understanding of the child. Children can't always see over a long period of time[40].

It is even ok for children to learn how their parents deal with them, and expect that if the other child gets something then their parents will try to compensate them. It isn't a rule[41] of the parents, rather it is from the parents' generosity.

---

[40] Adults sometimes also have that challenge.

[41] They will of course feel sad if the parents are unable to compensate them in a given situation, just like they would be sad if a parent was not able to provide any other thing which the child enjoys and the parents do their best to provide. Parents who are sensitive to their children's pain will try to ensure that they always have things available to compensate them so they will not experience that sadness.

If a grandparent offers to treat one child because they have a preference for that child, then the parents should tell the grandparents that it doesn't seem fair to the sibling. If they would take both but one child is unable to go, then the parents should let that child go and treat the sibling to something which they are able to go to. The sibling will understand somewhat, even though they do not understand fully. Parents have to know their children, and know whether they will be able to deal with not going when a sibling goes.

Sometimes children are not consoled. They don't understand and make a ruckus. They will tantrum or mope. They will learn that life doesn't always give you what you want.

Q: What should I do about my different-age children having different bedtimes?
Dr G: That happens. The only real answer is "When you get to be that age, you can do it also. Now it is not suitable for you."

Chapter 11

Children Helping in the House

Usually parents feel that children are *obligated* to help in the house. We wouldn't command a guest to help clean up after he ate at our table, or spent time in the living room. But with children, parents expect them to help with chores. If they resist, then parents make it into a power struggle.

Children are more helpful when they are treated as adults, when their self-autonomy is respected.

Children are people, and the more we treat them with unconditional love, and unconditional respect, the more they will become worthy of respect.

Why should children help

There are three reasons why parents think that children should help in the house. They think that it is the children's responsibility, they think that they need to be taught the idea of cleanliness, and think that they need to be *taught* to be kind and helpful.

Children's responsibility

It is not a child's responsibility to care for and clean up after themselves. Children are like guests in their parent's house. It is the parent's responsibility to care for their children while they are in the parent's house.

Even if children were responsible to care for and clean up after themselves, parents should not tell them to. Children are not born with a sense of responsibility. If they are forced to 'fulfill their responsibility,' and are treated negatively if they do not, it will create guilt and negativity within themselves for not wanting to do what they are told they should, though they don't recognize this responsibility. Like all Middos, the sense of responsibility will come with time and through the modeling of their parents. [see '**The Essence of Chinuch**']

Learning to keep clean

When parents model the middah of cleanliness, and are conscientious about cleaning up the messes they make and the messes of others, then children learn to do so themselves. If parents are indifferent, then children will be indifferent as well. Neat parents have neat children. Children will themselves feel that dirty things are yucky. It comes through time and modeling.

Learning to be kind and helpful

The middah of recognizing that their parents are working hard, and wanting to help their parents, is the middah of chesed. It grows with time and through modeling. It does not help to *force* children to mimic the act.

Parents should certainly not ask their children to help around the house to make it easier for *themselves*. Being *meshabed* [forcing labor on] children creates resistance. It serves no purpose, it results in fighting, and the task will only take longer for the parents to accomplish. It leaves a bitter taste and it can cause a power struggle. It is very sad if parents feel that they cannot manage without the help of their children. Children don't want to help that way. It is not a nice situation.

In a house where there is a housekeeper who cleans up after the *parents*, the children will have no model to learn from and will not learn to clean up after themselves. However, if the housekeeper cleans up after the children, but the parents *themselves* clean up the mess which they make, then the children will learn from the parents and as they get older will internally grow their middah of cleanliness. Of course, children should be given opportunities to practice expressing their middos in situations which they will enjoy.

Q: Should one ask their child to clean up what they used?
Dr G: Clean up? Why?
In general, it is looking for trouble to ask children to clean up.
In terms of chinuch to clean up after oneself, if you clean up, and your wife does, then your children will also when they are grown up. [See **'The Essence of Chinuch'**]

No one likes to clean up. Ask your child to close the door to their room if you don't enjoy seeing what is inside.

Q: What about Pesach cleaning?
Dr G: No one likes Pesach cleaning. Every Rabbi tells every person that Pesach cleaning is different from spring cleaning. Pesach cleaning is only a minimal cleaning. One should do spring cleaning at a different time. No one listens to the Rabbi. The worst thing is to force it on the children, to scratch out crumbs.

At a certain age, children will be appreciative of their parents, and view running the home as a *shutfus* [partnership], and will help out on their own.

Offering opportunities for chesed

There are times when children will want to help. Sometimes the task is fun to do. Sometimes one can offer a child a task that is 'beyond their age,' making the child feel grown up. Sometimes it is enjoyable to do something together with Mommy. Even if it is fun, they may not want to do it just then. If there is any element of force to it, then it is not a good idea. Children can be very helpful if they want to. Girls can bake a hundred pies for an affair. Boys can help build something. They feel very grown up and useful.

Children, when they get older and if they are not forced, get almost 'anxious' to help. They have the middah of chesed, of emulating Hashem. When they are able to see that their parent could use help, they pitch in. They volunteer to help and feel happy about it.

When children get older, parents can ask the child, without any aspect of forcing, 'would you mind helping out.' If it is fun or they feel grown up, together with their growing middah of chesed, they may be happy to. It is beneficial in cultivating their middah of chesed to offer them opportunities which they will be happy to do. One should only offer them an opportunity, if they might want to do it (either because they enjoy it or because they want to help). One can offer a young child to use the vacuum if that is fun for them. It is an opportunity to use their growing middah of chesed and cleanliness.

Managing the mess

Q: Children under two years of age make a big mess. They can't play in such a big mess.

Dr G: There should be a place for every toy. As each toy is finished being played with, parents should say 'Let's put it away together and then we will take out the next toy.' It is cooperative and fun. Often parents don't do that. One has to be on top of it. This is one of the difficulties of keeping a home straight; mess accumulates unless one is on top of it.

Parents should certainly not force children to clean up, but if the routine is that the first toy is cleaned up before a second toy is taken out, then children know that the next one won't come out until the first is cleaned up, and will frequently be happy to help their parents. It won't be viewed by the child as slavery, since it is being done with the parents. If the child doesn't want to help, the parents should not force them, and should do it themselves. This creates a habit[42] of *seder* [orderliness] which is good for children.

---

[42] The middah of Seder is unique. See **Essence of Chinuch** footnote on this topic.

Chapter 12

Teaching a Child to Speak Nicely

Using the words 'please' and 'thank you' when speaking to another person is a way of expressing one's feelings. They involve the middah of gratitude, and acknowledge the hardship one is requesting of the other person. Like all middos, when they are forced on children, children will reject them.

The words themselves lose their meaning when forced on children. Children think of the words as 'a meaningless formula you must use to be *machnia* [to humble] yourself, or else you will receive disapproval.'

The true meaning of 'please' is a way of expressing a request; it is a recognition of the hardship being imposed on the other person in order to fulfill that request. It also means that one is truly just as happy with either answer (yes or no).

The proper way to teach children the meaning of 'please' is by using it correctly. Do not misuse the word. Parents should not say 'please' if they are issuing a command. Parents constantly misuse the word 'please.' They order children around using 'please.' If the child refuses, the parents say "What!? You said no!?" If one uses 'please' as a command, children will understand it that way. Usually children misinterpret 'please' to mean a command.

The correct way to teach the usage of 'please' is for parents to say it themselves, and use it correctly. Children will pick up the meaning from seeing a wife say 'please' to her husband, and seeing him sometimes politely refusing. If parents want a child to do something which they don't have to do, they say 'please.' If the child indicates 'no,' then say 'That is okay.' Children will learn the meaning of 'please.' If parents respect children, then they will use the word 'please' when the child doesn't have to do something. Then children will understand its meaning. The usage of 'please' acknowledges the hardship involved.

Being polite is the middah of respecting someone else's dignity, it isn't an arbitrary set of words to use simply to be nice.

Q: I know that if my children don't say 'please' and 'thank you' to certain people, they will get negativity from them. Should I tell my children to say it just to those people, to avoid them getting that negativity?
Dr G: No. The children will be fine. Children realize that the aunt will disappear and that their parents are the meaningful ones. One also needn't say anything to the aunt; it is not necessary to educate other adults in the ways of raising children.

Q: What if the aunt is not frum, and she will get an incorrect impression about Judaism?
Dr G: Even if the aunt is not frum, we have more of an obligation to the welfare of our children than we do to other people.

Chapter 13

Temper Tantrums
and Time-outs

Dealing with temper tantrums requires an understanding of what is motivating the tantrum. In general, there are two reasons why children will have a tantrum. With very little children a tantrum is almost always because the child is unable to handle the situation and falls apart. Older children, starting at around three-and-a-half years of age, may be using a tantrum as a way to be obnoxious in order to manipulate their parents to do what they want. These two situations should be dealt with in different ways, and parents can tell from the situation why the child is throwing a fit.

Tantrum from a child losing control

When little children have tantrums, it is usually because they are not able to handle the situation. It can happen when *anything* doesn't go according to their expectations. Perhaps they are overtired, or they are hungry[43]. Punishing them for that doesn't accomplish anything, it only makes the situation worse. The best thing to do in that moment is to put them on your lap and soothe them[44]. That lets them know that Mommy is here, and Mommy will take care of them. If they are hungry then that may be why they are grumpy, so give them something to eat. Try to offer them an alternative to what they expected, chocolate syrup on vanilla ice cream may suffice for the chocolate ice cream they expected. After soothing them, distract them with something else fun.

Q: Maybe a little child also is trying to manipulate the parent?
Dr G: A little child is usually not that clever. Parents can tell by the situation.

Tantrum to manipulate; Refusal to listen to necessary instructions

Above the age of three-and-a-half, children may be using tantrums as a technique to be obnoxious in order to get their way.

Children learn quickly that crying isn't just an expression of emotion, it is also a tool that can be used to manipulate parents. It can start as an expression, and that changes into manipulation. While it may initially be a manipulative way to make the parents respond in a way that pleases the child, it can then turn into a method of achieving constant attention. It can also be enjoyable for the child to gain control over an adult.

---

[43] Sometimes adults also lose control of themselves in situations that are too much for them to properly process. There too, they should be relieved of their responsibilities so they can go calm down and regain their equilibrium.

[44] [See **Pacifiers During the Day**] This soothing is different than a child having a security blanket constantly available and running to it anytime they hit a bump (like an older child calling them a name which can happen frequently). This is an extreme situation where they melt down, and they need an escape to calm down. Sitting on a parent's lap and feeling their support is more effective than a security blanket.

In the end the child doesn't like it either. The child is unhappy, and the mother is unhappy. The child is acting in an unhappy way to achieve a result, but remains that way despite not achieving the result. The child does not realize that they will be happier if they stop.

Sometimes a child wants something for supper and it isn't available, and the parents are not able to get it. If the child starts to tantrum, the best thing to do would be to ignore it and let the child dissolve into tears. Then soothe the child and distract them, or offer an alternative.

The problem with ignoring children is that children don't want to be ignored. They will usually behave obnoxiously; hitting the parents, screaming, and bothering their siblings.
There are other situations where children must accept the authority of their parents[45]. Parents cannot have children staying up until eleven at night. Certain things are not livable for the welfare of the child. In this case, the parents have to assert their authority. The parents run the house. We listen to the children's requests, but, in the end, there are no negotiations.

A time-out is a good way to deal with these situations. The whole idea of a time-out isn't to punish children, it is to remove them from a reinforcing situation, thereby helping the child have quiet time to settle down, so they can think about and accept reality. "If you want to be a citizen, you have to follow the rules. Parents are the authority. They will listen to your perspective but they make the decisions. You must accept that 'balance.'" It is a form of coercing children, but it is the most mild form and it is necessary.

---

[45] It is not always necessary to coerce children into listening. If a child is refusing to come to dinner, they will learn the hard way that they will be hungry if they don't come to dinner. [See **Routine and Structure**]. However, the cases being discussed are situations where parents must have children accept their authority.

A time-out (enforced by locking the door to the room if they won't stay in) should be as many minutes as years the child is old[46], plus any additional time required until they are able to accept their parent's authority.

Q: Is it normal if once a day I have a situation where I feel the need to give my child a time-out?
Dr G: It could be. Some children are very stubborn. We are *Am k'shei oref* [a stubborn nation].
A person has to look at the type of situations. If they are all on the same issue, maybe the parents need a different approach. It is not so unusual for that to be necessary for a particular child.

Preventing the need for time-outs; Alternative

Q: How can one *prevent* tantrums?
Dr G: Try to make your home not a dictatorship, and take into account the feelings and needs of children. Children follow a leader who is good to them. Understand where a child is coming from, and what their thoughts and needs are. Be careful to say yes as much as possible, and be generous. As much as possible, make each situation for the child useful and enjoyable. Transitions are hard. Sometimes children are engrossed in what they are doing, when *you* are ready to serve supper. Maybe push off supper, or make going to supper something they look forward to. Try to make everything run smoothly, like a good nursery school.

---

[46] It is not an exact science, it is a rule of thumb. Studies show that children will promise to act properly in order to end a time-out, and then continue in the same way as before, as soon as they are out. As children get older they have more patience and a longer time perspective, so more time is needed in order for the time-out to have an effect on them.

Q: What about when my child has a meltdown in Wasserman's grocery store? There isn't a way for me to give them a time-out there, and they are trying to manipulate me. Can I leave them and walk away?

Dr G: You can do that. We did that sometimes. The child will be scared and will come along. 'I'm not going;' 'Okay, I am going.' The child will run after you as soon as you turn the corner. A person has to judge the situation.

If it is a younger child who isn't able to cope with something, then one should hold them in their lap and soothe them.

Q: What is the best thing to do about tantrums in stores?

Dr G: The best thing to do is to not take children to a store at all! Like the song says.

If you must take them, the best thing is to keep the child restrained and busy. Seat them in the basket with something to play with. Don't ignore the child, keep them busy with the play materials you brought. Children do very well with black and white. You can tell them 'If you're well behaved, you can take a candy from that shelf when we are finished getting the things we need.' It is very boring for a child to go shopping. If they are getting nothing out of it, they can be resentful.

Chapter 14

When to Hit a Child

Q: When should parents hit a child?

Dr G: The simple answer is *'never.'* Usually when parents hit a child, it is based on the wrong motives. Of course, a person should not hurt a child for anything that isn't a *sakana* [a concern of death], and certainly should not hit a child out of frustration.

Children learn from being hit that when people are big bullies, they can force others to do what they want by causing them pain. Children will not understand *why* they were hit, all they will know is that it is because the parent did not like what they were doing.

The idea of hitting a child in order to avoid danger

The Rosh HaYeshiva zt"l said that one *should* hit children to prevent them from causing a sakana. Running into the street, getting close to a fire, or biting another person (the mouth has organisms which could go into an open wound), which is a sakana for the *other* person, qualify for that situation. However, it is hard to get parents to hit children properly.

My father knew how to hit: my mother kept telling me to not run in the street, I didn't understand the danger at my age, so I ran into the street. My father grabbed me, he immediately pulled my pants down and gave me a big wallop. It was very unexpected from such a gentle person. My father let me stew in my misery before distracting me with something. He never apologized. The result was that I never ran in the street and he never hit me again.

When parents deliver a proper hit, they should not validate or commiserate with their child afterwards as it gives the child a mixed message. The child will get confused about whether the parent approves or doesn't approve of how the child acted. They shouldn't ignore the child for the rest of the day, but they should let the child digest what happened, and then distract them with something else.

There are certain things which justify traumatizing a child.

The trouble is that parents, especially women, are unlikely to hit well enough. The younger the child is, it makes it even harder. It is very hard for parents to traumatize a cute, cuddly one-year-old. Modern parents don't traumatize their children. Even my mother wouldn't hit me that way. I have never known a parent who successfully stopped their child from doing these things by hitting them.

It is better to avoid being in a situation where a parent would have to respond by hitting, since it is hard to respond properly. When we walked, our rule was that a child must either sit in the stroller, or hold on to the stroller. I cringe when I see a child at the corner and the mother is halfway down the block screaming at the child to stop.

The problem with doing it wrong is that children won't stop going in the street, and they will learn to hit others. Children will learn that it is a good way of inflicting pain. It is a power thing; they can get people to do what they want, or cause pain to others.

Q: Would a proper hit work for a very young child?

Dr G: One could traumatize a child even below the age of two, but parents would have to do it right, which modern parents don't.

Q: My two-year-old and one-year-old are biting and hitting over toys. What should I do?
Dr G: Separate them. They can't play together if one is biting the other.
One can use a gate to separate the playroom into two halves.
Some children bite and hit always, some only in specific circumstances. It is enjoyable for parents to be able to visit their siblings and shmooze, and they say "our children can even play together." However if the children don't play well together, then one should avoid visiting.

One has to understand that when children hit other children, it is usually for a reason.
Sometimes there is an older boy and a younger sister. The parents don't see; the girl hits the boy and the boy hits her back; he gets punished. Parents should ask: 'Why did he hit her?'
If she in fact didn't do anything, then maybe it is because the older child is jealous of the younger child. He was the center of the world, until his mother disappeared and then appeared with his competition. He could even love his younger sister sometimes; emotions can be contradictory. [see **Multiple Children**]

Q: If I am going to hit the child [against Rebbi's advice], can I add in that I am hitting them because they are hitting other children, in addition to biting?
Dr G: We don't want them to have terror for everything.
It is ok for a child to hit sometimes. A child could hit for fun, or sometimes for other reasons. Biting, however, is a sakana.

Using physical force

Q: What about man-handling a child, controlling them with physical force. Is there a place for that?

Dr G: There are times when it is important to man-handle a child. When a child must go to time-out, one does not negotiate. One has to separate the child so they can calm down until they can act like a social human. [See **Tantrums and Time-outs**]

If two brothers are play-fighting, let them enjoy it. If the fighting reaches the point of one of them possibly getting hurt[47] parents should separate them with physical force.

When one needs to change the diaper on a one-year-old, do the 'two-minute diaper change.' Or when getting them into a carseat. No one likes those things. Just do 'zoom zoom' and all done. [See **Physical Health of a Child**]

Dragging a child to the school bus is a hard way to start the school day. If parents have trouble getting a child to do a normal, regular routine, then they should question why it is so hard. If they are using positive anticipation and trying to make it run smoothly and happily and the child still doesn't want to do something regular, like going to the school bus, there may be a reason. Maybe the child is being bullied on the bus, or by the teacher in school. Parents should look into it.

Sometimes man-handling is an encroachment on their sense of Tzelem Elokim.

'Come here.' 'No.' 'What did you say??! I told you to come here!' 'Make me.' Then they shout and fight and there is injury to the child's self-esteem.

Try to make the day run smoothly and happily, like a good nursery school teacher. 'Come get dressed and then I can read to you' (not as a reward, rather because 'then I will have time'). [See **Building Self-Esteem in a Young Child**]

---

[47] Of course, parents should be 'on top of the situation' and tell the children to stop before it gets to that point. If they only notice that a fight has intensified after it has reached a possibility of injury, then they must use immediate action at that point in order to stop it.

Chapter 15

Physical Health of a Child

The general rule about ensuring children's physical health is that parents should find out what the child *needs*. If they *need* it, get it done with as much fun and as little pain as possible.

One should take children regularly to their health professional to have the child examined.

Find out what is going on with the child. If parents are concerned about a certain part of the child's diet, speak to a health professional. If there is an indication that there is a borderline serious concern, and there are foods that are known to cause that issue, then parents should cut down on those foods.

Food/Nutrition[48]

There has to be a sense of healthy balance between psychological wellbeing and parent's understanding of their children's physical wellbeing.

---

[48] [Also see Routine and Structure]

Some foods children don't like. One should be flexible in what children eat. Don't force them to eat certain foods. Children need to have a proper diet and proper nutrition. Find out what the child likes.

For some children sugar can cause hyperactivity. If it is true for a specific child, that the child really reacts to sugar, then one should take that into account. There is no such thing as 'all children' becoming hyperactive due to sugar. Some parents think all boys are hyperactive.

For girls, focusing on their weight too much can cause anorexia; it can cause them to feel guilty about eating.

Bathing

Some children perspire a lot, some don't. Different climates affect people differently. Sometimes children play in the dirt. Parents must ascertain if children need the bath.

There are ways to make baths more pleasant, such as bath toys or bubbles. Parents can be with the child, and they can play with them. Sometimes children just don't like baths. Sometimes it is due to a trauma or something similar; maybe they once read a story which affected them. But if the child needs it, the parents should get it done as painlessly as possible. Quickly in the bath, standing up, quickly pour water and then some soap and shampoo, quickly pour more water and done. The child may be screaming, but at least it was done very quickly.

Naps

Everyone likes children to nap, especially babysitters.
The important thing is how much sleep does the child have total in the day. That means calculating the time at night plus naps. Are they

getting the necessary hours? If they are sleeping through the night, they may not need much in the way of naps. Under the age of one, between twelve to fourteen hours of sleep daily is normal. One doesn't want children asleep most of their lives. It is a problem when one forces unnecessary sleep on little children. It is a concern if they sleep too much, or if they sleep too little. Ask a health professional if they are getting the proper amount. If the child needs it then parents must ensure they get it.

The problem with getting children to sleep during nap time is that nap times are variable. There are various ways to get them to sleep during the day. Typically, if children are exhausted, they will sleep.
Sleeping during the day is different from sleeping at night. (See **Sleep-Training**) One can put a baby in a stroller and rock the baby, or one can drive a baby in the car to get them to sleep.

Walking

Children like to walk. As soon as their muscles are developed they are anxious to walk, they try to stand up. It is one of the joys of parenthood, a good time for parents. One needn't try to push their children to walk. Sometimes children don't walk or talk because their muscles aren't ready. It *is* true that children who are significantly delayed in walking or talking might require speech or occupational therapy.

Summary

One can fight and stew and make a battle out of almost anything. However, most things can be designed so that children will enjoy them, and one can avoid causing the child pain while also ensuring their physical well-being.

Chapter 16

Shabbos

Muktzah toys

Q: Children don't like Shabbos because there is no technology. How does a parent encourage a child to like Shabbos?
Dr G: What we did was we had special Shabbos toys. Before Shabbos, we would take out the Shabbos toys, and put away the muktzeh toys.

Q: But they ask for the weekday toys.
Dr G: It must be black and white. There must be no deviations from the system.
Then they will know that this is how it is and they won't ask for the other toys.

Another purpose of Shabbos toys is to get rid of the possibility of children playing with toys that are muktzeh. It is best to make the problem disappear.

Children's divrei Torah

When our children were younger we had a rule 'You can't just read it. When you want to say it, put the paper away and say what you understand.' Children want to share, but this avoids them getting into the habit of saying things that they don't understand.

Kiddush

It is valuable for parents to make 'listening to kiddush' something their children will enjoy. Some ideas for how parents can do that is by letting children open the bottle, letting them say their own kiddush, or letting them drink from their own silver kiddush cup.

It is good for children to have a good association with kiddush at the table with their daddy and mommy; however, parents shouldn't *force* children to be there. Most children will like to be there anyway.

It is beneficial that 'kiddush with daddy and mommy' be enjoyable both for the family relationship and for the spiritual benefit. Eventually children will learn what Shabbos is really all about and they will connect that to their positive feelings about it. Parents should try to give the association that it is special to be a Jew. Even without the part of listening to kiddush, it is good that children enjoy the Shabbos table so that they will have positive associations about Judaism and Jewish things, even without necessarily understanding them. The understanding will come later.

Having children be quiet for kiddush when others are not able to hear properly to fulfill their mitzvah can sometimes be a challenge. A good idea can be to say kiddush in a louder voice. Parents can also try to give children the wine *before* kiddush.

Chapter 17

Stories of Gedolim

The right kind of parsha stories are nice. They can convey certain ideas about what a tzadik is, and present goals to strive for. Sometimes children enjoy the stories they are told, but sometimes they are waiting to leave the table. The good ones are few and far between. Most are too pedantic, and are not fun or relatable. The stories don't describe children like the ones who are listening, and the stories voice expectations that are beyond the abilities of the children listening. It depends on whether the stories convey a concept without getting preachy. The pirate books (by Rabbi Baruch Chait) are good for any age.

Q: Is it a good idea to have pictures of gedolim in one's house, and to tell stories of them, to set the tone of what greatness is? For example, the story with the water carrier and the Chofetz Chaim[49].

Dr G: They are 'plastic gedolim;' good stories have to be relatable. The story of the water carrier is too hard to relate to. First of all, what is a water carrier? The proper stories should be something which is easily understood. Avraham running at his age to feed strangers? Who

---

[49] As a child, he went out repeatedly in the cold to pour water out of the water-carrier's buckets which other children had filled as a prank, intending them to freeze overnight.

have we seen make extra doors so guests don't have to walk around to enter our house?

It has to be something relatable, if not to the child in their current state, at least to something which they can imagine reaching some day. The ability to do those actions is way beyond anything we see. To be inspiring it has to connect to the listener. It doesn't have to be getting up in the middle of the night. Rivka at the well is also hard to relate to; a three-year-old filling many pitchers of water for a stranger? People frequently speak over children's heads.

One could tell these stories if they are presented very simply. "A special girl Rivka gave a stranger a lot of water," "A special man Avraham invited guests over even when it was very hard for him."

Even for adults these stories are hard to relate to, but one could view them as contributing to the picture of Hashem's love for us as children of people who acted almost like מלאכים [angels].

Chapter 18

Sleep Training

Why should I sleep-train my child?

Sleep-training is a misnomer. Before a child is born (as any mother can tell you), a child knows how to put themselves to sleep and stay asleep. Going to sleep and staying asleep is not something that needs to be learned or 'trained.' However, shortly after birth, children learn something that, for good reason, becomes very important to them. Children learn that crying produces a mother. This is obviously very important and in children's best interests, however in their youth they make a mistake. Why should a child go to sleep, when they can get attention from their mother; all they must do is cry.

A common trap for parents is that while attempting to put their baby to sleep, when the baby cries the mother picks up and cuddles the baby to calm them and then attempts to put the baby to sleep again. At that point the baby cries again and the mother once again picks up the baby to cuddle and calm the baby, and the cycle continues. A common result of this, which is very unfortunate, is that parents can become cranky, and they can become angry at the baby (which they will then feel guilty about). The baby's sleep won't be good and the parents' sleep won't be good.

This is a classic example of where misplaced compassion is actually cruelty. Every child has a natural desire to cuddle and be with their mother, which is not bad, but it is an enjoyment which is short-lived. However, if the child sleeps through the night the child will be happier in the end.

Another goal of sleep training is to help children ignore stimulation (ie. sleep through wet diapers, teething, etc.). This allows the child to become a deep sleeper, which is good for their health.

The longer parents wait to sleep train, the harder it is to re-teach the child. Once a child can climb out of their crib it becomes even harder, because then parents will need a different barrier than the crib (like locking the door, if that can work. Sometimes children will destroy the room when that is the barrier.) The younger the child is, the better it is for the child and the parents. The best is to get it over and done with.

When is it appropriate to sleep train

Sleep training takes a lot of willpower. If parents go in when they shouldn't, all the previously ignored crying will have been for naught, as it will no longer be part of a beneficial procedure for the child; and letting a child cry without a valid reason is cruel. Before parents try it they must *make sure* they will be able to follow through.

When a baby comes home from the hospital, parents should look the baby in the eye in a serious way and say: "Now look you, you sweet little one. Before you were born you put yourself to sleep and stayed asleep for three hours. You're not going to take advantage of us."

On Day Two, the day a baby comes home from the hospital, a child can be expected to fall asleep and stay asleep for close to four hours. No baby needs to be fed more than every three to four hours (excluding extreme medical conditions).

How to sleep train

The crucial part is that parents should 'put the baby down and run,' and stay away for the length of time that the baby is currently capable of sleeping. Even if the baby cries before going to sleep or after waking up, parents should *not* go in. Through utilizing this method, the baby will realize that crying isn't an effective way to produce their parents *during sleep time*.

Starting at birth, one should feed and burp the baby, cuddle a little; do a quick bedtime routine, then put the baby in and run!

Q: What if the baby cries after two and a half hours, should the parents service the baby then?
Dr G: It really should be four hours, or close to it. Two and a half hours is only close to three. Let the baby cry until another hour has passed.

Q: When should a person give in? What if a baby is screaming for an hour?
Dr G: An hour of screaming is nothing! We are *am keshei oref* [a stubborn nation].
If you set a limit for how long you will let the baby cry, the baby will exceed it and then it will become a battle of willpower each time. By not going in, the baby will realize that crying is not effective to produce their parents during sleep time. The human biological clock is very precise and they will learn to sleep during their sleep time.

Q: Is it okay for a baby to cry for that long? Isn't it unhealthy for the baby?
Dr G: Crying is a natural thing. When children lose their breath, the brain quickly reacts and they get their breath back.

At birth babies can stay asleep for close to four hours. As children grow it will become five and then six hours. In principle, at twelve weeks old and at twelve pounds babies can sleep for twelve hours as they have enough nutrition for the entire night; however one can start with nine or ten hours. Parents should pick a bedtime, then let the baby sleep for ten hours. When the baby cries after those ten hours, the parents should attend to the baby's needs. Smart parents will put a baby to sleep at a time when the end of the ten or twelve hours coincides with when the parents *want* the baby to wake up.

The general rule is that whatever a baby *does* one third of the time, they can be *held to* all the time, as it indicates that they are truly capable of sleeping for that long. When a baby can sleep for six hours, then parents should hold the baby to six hours, or no more than servicing the baby once a night (it does not have to be exactly at the six hour mark, it could be shortly before).

Sleep training specifics and advice

Sometimes there is a specific problem and therefore the sleep training is not working. If parents have tried for a week, or a week and a half, and it isn't working, they should speak to someone with experience, like a health professional, to help figure out what the cause is.

Children suffer from sleeping away from home in various ways. Parents should not start sleep-training the child if they know that they will be traveling before the child will be well-trained. Before going away, the best thing is to have a couple of weeks at home, so the child will have a solid *kinyan* [hold] on sleep training. Then when the family returns home, the pattern will return faster. If the child is already trained but the pattern is broken, parents *will* have to retrain the child, but it will be easier.

Children should not be given a pacifier; using a pacifier has big disadvantages. If children get used to stimulation, then their sleep will not be as deep. It would certainly be bad if it ends up as a 'game of fetch' with the parents feeling driven to get the pacifier when the pacifier falls out (though anyway they should not be going in *at all* during the child's 'sleep time'). If the pacifier is only used to help the child fall asleep, but then it is taken away, it could work.[50]

It is not necessary to rock children to sleep; before they were born they fell asleep without it.
It is not necessary to nurse a child to sleep, but it is okay. But then put the baby down and run! The idea is not to nurse them until they are asleep, rather it is a fine way of calming them, it is a bedtime routine[51]. If they aren't interested in nursing they should still be put down to sleep. If the mother is in the middle of nursing, and a child falls asleep, or if it is their bedtime, they should be put to sleep and they don't need the entire nutrition.[52]

Sick children sometimes need special attention during the night and *should* be attended to.
If children are sick with a cold or a cough the parents can put them in a car seat (so the nose discharge doesn't stuff up their nose), even though in general it is not a good idea to have children sleep in a car seat.

It is a good idea to burp the baby after feeding because the gas will wake the baby up. Feed, and burp, then put the baby down.

Children who are teething can still sleep. If they couldn't, they wouldn't sleep throughout childhood (children are always teething). Before they go to sleep try to put something on their gums to remove some of the pain, but don't come to them in the middle of the night.

---

[50] Anyway, leaving a pacifier in while children are sleeping is bad for their teeth. A bottle of milk is even worse. The milk stays in their mouth and bacteria love milk.

[51] It is fine for a child to be dependent on a calming bedtime routine before going to sleep. The only problem is when they are dependent on something to get them to actually fall asleep.

[52] If one wants a child to get the whole feeding, they can obviously start feeding earlier so the child can complete it before falling asleep.

If a child has a dirty diaper and wakes up then they should be changed, however parents should not be constantly 'checking on them.' If the child sleeps through it, let them be.[53]

It is best that children's rooms should be completely dark. All dark rooms are the same and they will not be as uncomfortable if they are switched to a different room when one has to sleep away from home. Another advantage of having the light off is that when children grow older they can get scared of 'scary things' they see in the room if there is something they can 'see.' A third benefit is that they cannot find entertainment near them such as toys or pacifiers.[54] In addition, if the source of light is a door ajar, children will more frequently be able to hear their parents walking around, and will feel that their parents are neglecting them when they cry. A dark room with the door fully closed is a clear signal that it is sleeping time. There *is* a benefit for children to be able to sleep in rooms that are not completely dark, but that benefit is outweighed by the losses.

Waking up siblings is a problem. The best is when a baby is in a room with no one else. Sometimes parents can start the baby off in the parent's bedroom and then when the parents go to sleep, they can move the baby to a far corner of the house.

Bathing is fine before bedtime, if you can do it every day. It is soothing for children. If it is within an hour of bedtime, but isn't every day, then it is inconsistent and it is confusing for children. They will want the enjoyable experience of their recent memory and will attempt to cry until they are given it. Giving a bath every other day before bedtime is also consistent, they will perceive the pattern, but a baby may need a bath on the odd day also. If a baby is dirty and needs a bath on any day that is not part of a consistent pattern, it would be better to give them the bath more than an hour before bedtime.

---

[53] Dirty diapers can cause rashes, and during the day they should be changed. Children should not be 'trained to ignore them.'

[54] Which really shouldn't be there regardless.

Swaddling can be helpful, depending on the child, if it works for them.

Daytime naps

Nap times are usually not so fixed. Often it is impractical and therefore often they are not done at the same time. Because of that it is hard to get children to go to sleep during a nap. Rocking children is good but takes a long time. There is value in not frustrating the parents and instead putting the child in a swing to get them to sleep.

Nursing a child to sleep can be a way to get them to sleep for a nap. When putting children to sleep for a nap, the point is not to have a long experience with the mother. Rather, just a short, conscious experience, and then go to sleep.

Q: Are we not concerned that they have to learn to fall asleep on their own?
Dr G: At night, yes one must be. During the daytime one has to be flexible due to the circumstances.

Even if children's nap schedules can be consistent, parents should first make sure that their night-time sleep training is down solid. If it is, they could try to sleep-train the child for day naps as well.

The best is if naps are at a set time. It is also important that it should be for a longer period of time. There is no point in letting a child scream for an hour if they only need an hour of sleep. They didn't fall asleep and were in pain for an hour. If they are picked up after an hour of crying, they will think that they were imposed upon, but escaped with their crying. They will *not* eventually realize that they won't get attention for the hour[55]. Even an hour-and-a-half is not a good idea,

---

[55] At night when they aren't picked up and they instead sleep, they do realize that the lack of attention is because this is sleeping time.

as children can scream for an hour[56] just to get a half hour of sleep. It is also important that if there is a babysitter involved, that they are willing to go along with the system. [See more about naps in **Physical Health of a Child**]

---

[56] At night they will eventually sleep for the whole time after a couple weeks. During the day, light and sounds can disturb their ability to get to and stay sleep, and this can happen even regularly. If the amount of time they slept was longer it could be worth it.

Chapter 19

Sexuality in Young Children

A person is born with sexuality. It is good for children to have it remain under the surface until the child matures physically and it emerges anyway. At that point the child will have the challenge of controlling their urges until they have the proper context in marriage.

Once the urges are stimulated, they tend to be hard to control. It can lead to serious problems of sz"l for boys, and for girls the difficulty in resisting opportunities to have a boyfriend.
One should avoid having the urge stimulated in children earlier than it would occur naturally.

Parents should never let children play too long by themselves with a child of the opposite gender. Parents who leave five- or six-year-olds together may walk in and be horrified by what they see. They should not be horrified, it is normal; but it should not be encouraged (one should avoid instigating it).
Children always must have a *mirsus* [fear of being walked in on].

If one discovers their child 'playing doctor' they should distract their child into another activity. It doesn't have to be made into a big deal, and *should not* be made into a big deal. Making it into a big deal can traumatize children and teach them that sexuality is terrible, which will hurt them later in life. Parents should do it in a way that children don't feel guilty about themselves.

Q: Do children know that Mommy will not like us doing this?
Dr G: It is a natural understanding[57]. They may lack the self-control to refrain from it. The important thing is that they always have a mirsus.

Q: Should a mother always walk in on young children? Won't they feel a lack of privacy, that she is busting in on them?
Dr G: Sure she should. Children expect that a parent will.
It is Mommy's house, she can go where she wants. If children are playing in a room, they expect that Mommy will walk in.

If two children get into the habit of 'playing doctor' for an extended period, such as for several weeks, they shouldn't be allowed to play together alone, without an adult there for six weeks.
Sometimes parents go too far, 'I'll never let my child play with that..." That is more than is necessary to prevent such behavior from recurring. After the six weeks, a parent should make sure to maintain a mirsus, as one should always have with children.

Sometimes little boys and little girls like to rub themselves on their private area. Don't stigmatize it. Don't repress it. Get them up and interested in doing something else.[58]

Young children of different genders taking baths together is fine until one child starts taking an interest in and exploring the other one. Then it is time for separate baths.

---

[57] It is possible that a child doesn't yet understand that what they are doing is wrong. A parent could say to a child one time ever, in a gentle way 'Don't do this kind of game, we keep our tushy covered' before distracting the child into an activity.

[58] For adults too, a person should deal with desires of Taavah by taking their mind off it by getting involved in another activity.

Q: The child explored, so then we took a break and gave them separate baths. Now can we go back to taking baths together?

Dr G: You can try again, maybe the urges went back under the surface again, but be attentive to them resurfacing.

Chapter 20

Pacifiers During the Day

When dealing with a little baby, there are two needs which a parent must satisfy. Babies have a need to be held, and they have a need to suck. Some of their need to suck is satisfied by nursing or bottles, but their need goes beyond that. If a baby is held and given a pacifier, that is good. That is for an infant; it is fine for one-year-olds to run around and play with a pacifier in their mouth.

A two-year-old will sometimes go for a pacifier or a security blanket when they encounter frustrating circumstances. This is not good because running away from frustration into *taavah* [physical pleasure] makes a person, to a degree, an addict to gratification; in this case oral gratification. It can lead to needing other oral stimulation to soothe oneself. It can lead to an addiction to food. Some adults, in particular those who are around the home a lot, frequently have snack food around and use it when frustrated.

Frustration means that there is something which the child wanted that didn't go well. They are trying to put a toy together and it doesn't go together. They want to climb on the furniture and their mother wouldn't let them. Sometimes it is social; for example if the child is insulted by a peer.

Sometimes children tantrum, sometimes they just mope and retreat. I'd much rather see a child get angry than see the child retreat. A child who gets angry is more motivated to be helped to find a solution to their frustration, and isn't practicing an unhealthy coping mechanism[59]. Children who retreat are acting in an unhealthy manner in response to their challenges, and are also less motivated to be helped to find a solution.

Parents should make security items like pacifiers, blankets, and anything else[60] which children use to soothe themselves, unavailable to children during the day. By removing their soothing escape, it will force a different solution.

The best is if parents can deal with the child's frustration by addressing the problem. For example, a common case of a child who is bullied can be helped by building up their sense of self[61]. Child: 'My brother called me a dum-dum.' Parent: 'You know you're not a dum-dum. You know he's just trying to get you upset. Now go play and if he calls you a dum-dum, tell him he is a mum-head.'

Some children don't have the ability to express themselves in a way that parents can interpret and help them to deal with their frustration. In that case, try to get the child up and interested in another activity.[62]

Q: Are teddy bears the same thing as sucking a pacifier in that they soothe children when they are frustrated?

---

[59] Even if parents are unable to help them find a solution, at least they aren't learning to escape their discomfort with taavah.

[60] A sippy cup is a bottle. There is no purpose to a sippy cup. If a child is young enough that they cannot drink from a regular cup, give them a bottle. One can avoid developing a potential security item by giving children regular cups when they no longer need bottles.

[61] [Also see **Dealing with Multiple Children** 'Children Fighting']

[62] In general, that is the way to deal with the desire to soothe oneself with Taavah, even for adults. Don't stigmatize them, don't repress it. Get up and do something interesting.

Dr G: Teddy bears aren't necessarily the same problem. It depends how they are used.

When children pick them up if they are frustrated, it could be. For some children they are lively things to play with.

Q: What about using a pacifier when children are going to sleep?

Dr G: [See '**Sleep-Training**' for more, as relevant to using a soothing item to fall asleep] Going to sleep is a little different. Having a calming thing is not so bad, if used at a time when a person needs to escape into a state of calmness. There is a need for the body and the mind to escape the stresses of the world and retreat into fantasies, to escape into a retreat from the world. Who is *not* dependent on something soothing, such as a soft blanket, to fall asleep? It is not necessarily a bad thing if it is limited to sleep time.[63]

---

[63] [See **Temper Tantrums and Time-outs** for another exception when soothing a child from a painful experience is healthy]

Made in the USA
Columbia, SC
15 November 2024

e9f2dc30-ab89-404b-baa5-c01853583c8fR01